# MISS OLMSTED'S NORMANDY INN

## PAMELA LEE

Tigerlily Farm Productions, LLC

# *DEDICATION*

Terri Sanford

Miss Olmsted's Normandy Inn was created due to my friend Terri Sanford's curiosity about the history of her building. This book is dedicated to Terri. She has always been there when I needed her the most. Many people benefit from Terri's kindness and gentle spirit, just as I have.

My Grandmothers

This book is also dedicated to my grandmother, Marguerite Brill Wilson, and great grandmother, Maude Woodhouse Brill, two wonderful and strong ladies that lived through World War I, Women's First Right to Vote, Polio Epidemic, the Great Depression and World War II. They told me stories about their lifetime experiences and I selected some to share with you, dear reader.

# Acknowledgements

Thank you for research assistance of this book to Sandi Hamilton, President Town of Sodus Historical Society who helped me locate much of the history, people to interview and even found some potential recipes, and Edson Ennis, Wayne County Museum of History Board Member, for sharing artifacts, locating people to interview and telling me his funny stories.

A special thank you to those who agreed to be interviewed and described their experiences at the Normandy Inn; Betty DeMent, Donna D'Ercole Douglas, Pete and Jan Mastracy, Rita Kilpatrick, Amy Tindall, Miranda Almekinder, Jim Hoyt, Terri Sanford and Erin Atkins. All of you have helped keep this property going over the years, so that the community can continue to enjoy the building and history.

I am so very grateful for Mr. Stefan Uveges, former English Professor, for proof reading and offering suggestions to put polish on this project. You are the Best!

# Contents

# MISS OLMSTED'S
# NORMANDY INN

# I

# Establishing a Normandy, France Experience

The history of the Normandy Inn involves both a developed concept, as well as a physical location. Located in Sodus, New York, the building originated as a barn, then was used as a restaurant through three ownerships, an auction house/feed store and finally a feed store/artisan co-op. The rise to fame of the Normandy Inn requires the telling of the founder, Miss Katherine Olmsted, and the development of her business concept.

The Normandy Inn development story is unusual and it is important share before the facts are lost to time. Katherine Olmsted started out as a nurse during the first half of her career life and during the second half, created a new career as a Cordon Bleu Chef and owner of the Normandy Inn. In the process of pursuing her life's dream, she impacted an entire community with her kindness and provided employment to many families over a thirty-six year time span. This was not an easy task during the Great Depression when unemployment was high and people could not find work. Katherine's vision for the Normandy Inn became enormously popular and had far appeal, well throughout the states and beyond. She was a person who accomplished so much in one lifetime.

It is hopeful that others may find inspiration from the retelling of the story of Katherine Olmsted's life experience.

The story begins by summarizing Katherine Olmsted's early years. The Arms' Crossroads Wallington, compiled by the Wallington School-house Restoration Committee, does an excellent job in preserving the history of Katherine's younger days and also providing stories of local residents at that time.

> Katherine Olmsted was born and raised in Des Moines, Iowa. Her mother, Emma Lent Olmsted, was the daughter of Charles Lent, a successful fruit grower in Wallington, New York. Katherine's father was Augustus L. Olmsted, who managed a branch of the Olmsted Saddlery Company. Katherine's family visited her grandparents in Wallington each summer and later, Katherine herself would visit when on vacation from her nursing duties. (Wallington 1982, 68)

Katherine documented her education and nursing career choices in a resume, a copy of which is housed in her Red Cross Service file, found in the National Archives.

> Katherine applied to the Red Cross reserves in 1914. According to her Red Cross service file, housed at the National Archives, she was a very outspoken individual, especially when it came to making things right for the public she served. Katherine's service file is a mixed bag; peppered with reprimands from Red Cross staff, letters from Katherine requesting brochures to hand out, and requests from many organizations for her to speak at meetings/banquets. She was a real advocate for the people that she served and accomplished so much in every position she held. In July 1917, Katherine was finally tapped by the Red Cross to serve as a nurse, overseas in Roumania during World War I. Several months into this assignment, the unit of Red Cross nurses and doctors encountered a siege by

the Germans and escaped out of Russia to Murmansk, 150 miles above the Arctic Circle.

Following her return to the U.S. in May 1918, Katherine began lecturing and telling of her war time experiences for a few months. Afterwards, she returned to public health nursing. The Red Cross continued to offer her employment, especially overseas, but Katherine preferred to remain stateside. She was a sought after nurse and on February 26, 1919 the Red Cross Acting Director, Department of Nursing wrote, "We recognize Miss Olmsted as one who meets all our requirements and has shown capable of putting our message across in an intelligent and impressive manner. We are, therefore, very anxious to secure her service." In December 15, 1920, Katherine accepted the position of Director of Public Health Nursing with League of Red Cross Societies, in Geneva Switzerland. At the same time, she was offered a position as Assistant to Miss Hay, American Red Cross in Europe, which she declined. (National Archives 1978 file 1 of 2, 9-153)

"Katherine spent the next four years as Director of Public Health Nursing overseas, and traveled through fifty-two countries. In 1925 Katherine took a furlough to the U.S. for several months" (Recordings 1925, 4). "There are two speaking requests in Katherine's Red Cross file, anticipating if they are on the visit list and would like to have Miss Olmsted speak. Katherine informed Washington Head Quarters that she had 28 talks scheduled to various groups" (National Archives 1978 file 2 of 2, 94).

"Katherine and her mother traveled from Paris to Wallington before Christmas 1925 to begin the furlough, taking some time at home" (Recordings 1925, 4). "After six months, Katherine and her mother returned to Paris with her Aunt Kathryn Lent joining them in May 1926" (Recordings 1926, 4). Based on these quotes, it appears that Katherine, her Mother, Emma, and her two aunts, Mary and Kathryn, were all very close. Katherine's aunts were both nurses and this may have had an influence on Katherine's career choice.

Only a few months after returning to Europe, Katherine resigned from the Red Cross in 1926. Her resignation letter states in part, "Baroness Mannerheim has definitely requested that the Nursing Division of the League act as headquarters for the International Council of Nurses." The governing board of the European Council disagreed, and she states "therefore, I tender my resignation and sever all connection with the European Council for Nursing Education." (National Archives 1978 file 2 of 2, 103)

The tone of her resignation letter sounded angry that the Council disagreed with her proposition and she was completely done with her position. However, it was the end of her first career that allowed Katherine to direct her energy to her next career, which was "to create her own tea shop. After resigning the Red Cross, in 1926, Katherine enrolled in the University of the Sorbonne Cordon Bleu cooking school in Paris, before leaving Europe" (National Archives 1978 file 2 of 2, 49). She reinvented herself with a new purpose, to begin a new adventure in life. What she may have not known at this point in time is the huge impact her new purpose would have on an entire community, or that her venture would provide employment during the Great Depression, continuing for many people over the next 36 years.

To read more about Katherine's early nursing career, look for *Miss Olmsted's Nursing Adventure*, prequel book written by Pamela Lee with scheduled release date in early 2024.

Katherine Olmsted circa 1935
*Photo courtesy of Sodus Historical Society*

According to Anna Olmsted, Katherine's cousin, "the Cordon Bleu cooking course held at the University of the Sorbonne in Paris had a stiff schedule. Katherine watched demonstrations by master chefs and then practiced cooking from six a.m. until six p.m." (Olmsted, A. 1967, 18).

**Sorbonne University, Paris France early 1900's**
*sorbonne-universite.fr*

Le Cordon Bleu, Paris website describes the Cuisine Diploma as a comprehensive and rigorous training programme that allows the progressive learning of French culinary techniques. The programme is taught by Le Cordon Bleu Paris Chefs, who have worked in some of the world's finest restaurants. With the knowledge gained from a rigorous training, students who have completed the Diplome de cuisine will be ready for a career in a professional kitchen or embark on a career change in French cuisine. The course teaches French culinary techniques, classic dishes and regional French and European cuisines. Teaching method is comprised of demonstrations, practical classes and theory classes. Intake for applicants is four times a year; January,

April, July and October with duration is 6 months Intensive or 9 months Standard. (Cuisine Diploma-Paris 2023)

"The Record mentions Katherine's return with her Mother, Emma, and Aunt, Kathryn, upon completion of the Cordon Bleu course on February 25, 1927 to New York City where they stayed with Mary Lent, her aunt, and then they returned to Wallington on March 25, 1927" (Recordings 1927, 4). "The Arms' Crossroads Wallington mentions that Katherine returned from France with a young French chef named Fernand" (Wallington 1982, 71).

And apparently, they brought a lot of stuff with them to decorate the new tea shop. A Syracuse area newspaper reports, "the freight bill upon reaching the U.S. was nearly $1,000 in 1927" (VanWormer 1947, 24). The local paper provided a description of items.

They arrived with a large collection of French copper, pewter, brass, colorful pottery, china, French Provincial furniture and tapestries. Katherine brought with her marvelous European antiques, largely gifts from Queen Marie as a token of her deep appreciation for Olmsted's work in Rumania during the war. Among the items was a large collection of brass and copper cooking utensils, and heavy Polish and Rumanian cookware. These items would provide the atmosphere that reminded her so much of that of Normandy in France. ("Historic Normandy Inn" 1980, 5)

**Brass and Copper from Europe**
*Photo courtesy of Sodus Historical Society*

The change in careers from nursing to owning a tea shop is a vastly a different line of work. A nursing position involves working for a business versus owning your own business, as a tea shop proprietor. Preparing and serving meals is quite a divergence from training nurses and caring for ill people as well. However, after "Katherine's wartime experience in Romania, where meats, fats, butter, eggs and other necessities were scarce and Katherine lost over twenty pounds"(Interesting 1918, 6); perhaps owning a tea shop with plenty of food for everyone is not so difficult to understand. Hamilton B. Allen, a food critic from the Rochester area, mentions in his column that "he had been a customer of the Normandy Inn since the 1930s and his description below also provides a clue" (Allen 1968).

Allen stated that Katherine had become smitten with the charm of provincial France and the little family run dining rooms, which she discovered during post-Armistice travels that she decided to create, in her Lake Ontario homeland, a dining room which would recapture as nearly as possible the charm and flavor of the French originals which inspired her. (Allen, 1968)

"The local newspaper reports that Katherine opened the "Auberge N'ormande" her Tea Shop in June of 1927" ("Sodus Centre" 1927, 6). "Katherine started her business venture in an old dry house on her brother's, Harry, farm on Maxwell Creek. She then pursued her lifelong dream of bringing a little of Normandy, France to the United States" (Wallington 1982, 71).

Auberge means hotel or inn in French language. And so Auberge, N'ormande is the French pronunciation for Normandy Inn.

The dry mill on Harry Olmsted's farm, Katherine's first Normandy Inn

*Arms' Crossroads Wallington, The Wallington Cobblestone Schoolhouse Restoration Committee*

And thus, Katherine's business concept had begun and would continue to grow. In a lucky break,

> ...a year earlier in 1926, the United States began a numbered highway system. In a precursor to the modern interstate highway system, the federal government introduced a national highway numbering system in an effort to standardize roadways, especially local roads and trails with names unfamiliar to outsiders. The U.S. Numbered Highway System made it easier for the growing number of car owners to figure out how to get from one city or town to the next and opened the way for the great American road-trip tradition (Giuseppe 2020).

The highway numbering system helped customers find the tucked away Inn. Today, the street address for the Normandy Inn is 7639 Ridge Road, Sodus, New York. Back in 1927, Garmen had not been invented yet, or internet and Map Quest. Folks were dependent upon good old paper maps and road signs.

"At first, people came out of curiosity, but returned for the unique surroundings and excellent food. The dry house on her brother's farm was decorated as a French café, which held only 12 people" (Wallington 1982, 71). "The restaurant prospered. It was most beautiful when it was located in the dry house, complete with a yard full of white geese. The inn proved a great asset to the community during the depression years, at one time supporting about 35 families" ("Historic Normandy Inn" 1980, 5).

The community already knew Katherine well based on news articles published in The Record newspaper. Katherine was mentioned regularly over the years in The Record and her comings, goings, and speeches to local organizations are well documented. "The Record published a series of letters during her nursing experience in Europe during World War I and issued a front page interview and picture of Katherine in May 1918 when she returned. She was a local celebrity and the community rallied around her when she moved to Wallington and started her tea shop.

Their support was documented as her business grew" ("Miss Olmsted Returns" 1918, 1).

# 2

# A New Building

The Wallington Cobblestone Schoolhouse Restoration Committee provided an excellent summation of the beginning days and start-up of Katherine's new tea shop. The writers of that book refer to her as 'Katie', which may have been her locally known nickname in Wallington, as the local folks knew her since childhood.

Two years later, the Auberge N'ormandie had quickly outgrown the dry house and Katie began the search for a larger place. She settled on Mr. and Mrs. Veltman's home and old barn on the opposite (west) side of the creek. She personally supervised the remodeling of the barn to be used as her new Inn. The hayloft was converted to a dining balcony and a fireplace was added. Katie and her mother Emma lived in the small bungalow behind the barn. Visitors continued to be invited to gather in the parlor while waiting to be seated. An assortment of appetizers were provided to the guests, which encouraged a companionable atmosphere. This kindly entry made dining a real experience and not just a meal. (Wallington 1982, 71)

Parlor for appetizers 1929
*Picture courtesy of Sodus Historical Society*

Parlor with stairs to balcony and monk's chairs from monastery
*Picture courtesy of Sodus Historical Society*

**Dining Balcony 1929**
*Picture courtesy of Sodus Historical Society*

"It was at this time the name changed from the French pronunciation Auberge N'ormandie to the English pronunciation Normandy Inn, as reported in the "Record Jr." (1930, 8). "Normandy is a region in France along the north coast, with the English Channel separating it from England. The Atlantic Ocean feeds into the English Channel and provides ocean fish and shells, with long beaches along France's north coast" (Googlemaps, 2023). "Sea shells were used in Katherine's serving ware, as reported by multiple diners over the years. One of the signature dishes of the Normandy Inn was le Coquille St. Jacques, served on an ocean shell (DErcole 2023)."

And to compliment the new building, local waitresses donned peasant costumes, reminiscent of the Normandy France region, complete with kittles, or aprons, and caps. Many of the local youth were employed at the newly expanded Normandy Inn.

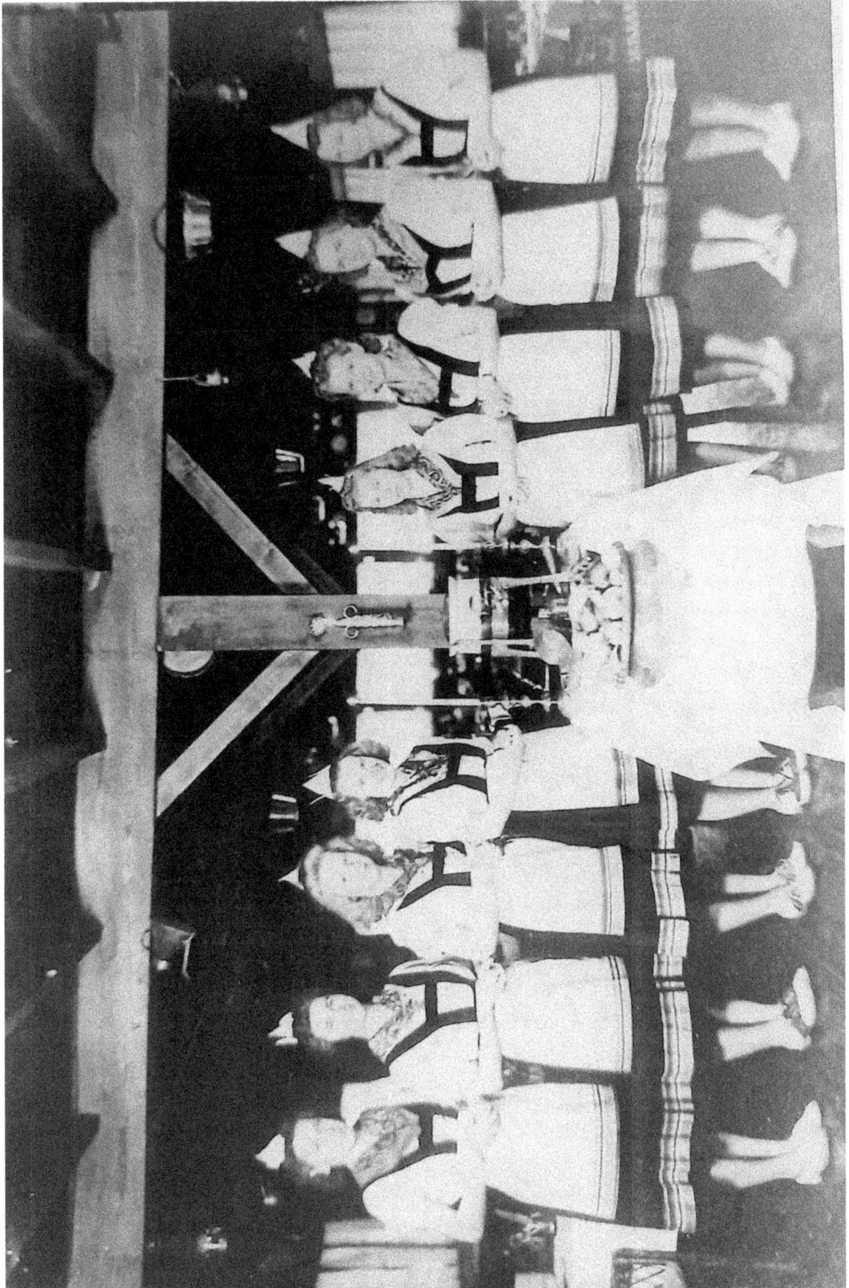

Uniformed waitresses in new dining hall 1929
*Picture courtesy of Sodus Historical Society*

In a local newspaper article by Grace Lynch, she recalls that "in the center of the Inn's front door was a large iron coat of arms, the double headed eagle with crown, which was from Czar Nicholas II's train obtained during Katherine's WWI service" (Lynch 1968).

**Iron Coat of Arms from Czar Nicholas II's Train**
*The Story of an American Red Cross Nurse, Anna W. Olmsted*

Katherine loved dogs and once sold pet food at the Normandy Inn. It is interesting that she also offered pet supply food at her dining establishment. The Record reported that "six police puppies were at Normandy Inn. Miss Olmsted said, "I spend most of my time playing with them. All dogs like puppy biscuit and Ken-L-Ration. You will find a fresh stock in our store" ("Record Jr." 1930, 8).

Katherine's Normandy Inn, tea shop, settled in the new old barn across the creek and she and her mother, Emma, settled in the small cottage, behind the barn. The description sounds an idyllic country setting.

**3**

⚬⚬⚬

# Time to Grow Again

**Normandy Inn front entrance, menu cover**
*Rita Kilpatrick private collection*

"The shield over the front door is the French Coat of Arms of Lorraine, according to VanWormer 1947." "The bell at the peak of the roof was from England is and powder coated, according to Donna D'Ercole Douglas, and was brought to Sodus by Katherine Olmsted." There is no other engraving on the bell.  It looks as if the bell is meant

18

to be pulled by a rope to ring, and may have announced school, church or meetings.

Katherine's Normandy Inn hosted people from the community for meetings and social gatherings, as outlined in this quote from the Arms' Crossroads-Wallington.

> Always particularly fond of children, Katie became involved in the social 4-H Club of Sodus, where she counseled and worked with the young. She also belonged to the Wayne County Home Bureau and often insisted that the meetings be held at her Inn.
>
> The Inn was now open from April through November and was used as a community center in the winter for parties, dances and social meetings. Attendees brought a dish to pass and many times Miss Olmsted donated coffee and meats if she was not at her winter retreat on Pine Island, Florida. One of the biggest social events of the year always on November 29 marked the annual closing fest. Everyone brought their dishes to pass and Katie laid out all the leftovers from the season. After a buffet dinner, the tables were pushed back, and young and old alike square danced into the wee hours of the morning, making it a real family fun night. (Wallington 1982, 75-76)

"Katherine's passion was the Normandy Inn first and fishing, second. She pursued fishing all winter long while in Florida" (Wallington 1982, 82). As mentioned previously, Katherine spent winters on Pine Island, Florida. According to Betty DeMent, former waitress, "Pine Island is great for fishing. Betty and her husband also spent winters on Pine Island, Florida, many years later in the late 1990's. Betty said they would take a boat out about 10 miles into the ocean and catch lots of flounder and other ocean fish" (DeMent, 2023).

The Normandy Inn was becoming a popular place, both with the locals and dinner guests. As the popularity grew, so did the building.

In 1932, a new wing was added to the end of the Inn, housing a large dining room. The central room that served as the dining room was converted into a parlor where the guests visited while waiting to for service. The new dining room was a community project, so it seemed only right that the Inn was used as a community center.

Aside from being able to serve more people, the reason for adding the large dining room was a desire expressed by the men saying they would like a bigger floor for dancing. So, one day the men showed up with several tractors, dragging timbers and railroad ties that they had stripped from an old trolley bridge, that Kathrine bought on the spur of the moment for $12 from a man who was determined to sell it to her.

But the Normandy Inn wasn't just the meeting place for the Wallington people, it also welcomed banquet dinners for clubs, faculty and business groups as well as wedding receptions.

The addition of the dining room proved to be a valuable asset, for that year, 1932, in eight months the Normandy Inn took in $38,000. (Williams 1937)

"Using an on line calculator and converting 1932 dollars to 2023, that amount is a whopping $829,815 in today's money" (Webster, March 2023).

Dining in elegance at the Normandy Inn in the newly added north
dining hall circa 1950
*Arm's Crossroads Wallington, The Wallington Cobblestone Schoolhouse Restoration
Committee*

Foyer of the Normandy Inn showing many of Miss Olmsted's
collectibles
*Donna D'Ercole Douglass*

A strong bond developed with area residents because the new party room was offered to them during the off season as a community center. The bond was demonstrated when one evening, after the restaurant had closed and all the help had left, two large busses carrying about a hundred college fraternity students pulled up in front of the Inn. They were sure that they had made reservations, but actually had not so and were very disappointed. Having plenty of food on hand, Olmsted said "come on in." She then telephoned a neighbor who blew the fire siren. "There isn't a fire," she said, "but this is an S.O.S. call" and enough help arrived to cook and serve dinner. Katherine's help was just that loyal and many local women returned every season to serve as cooks, and attractive young girls of the area returned to waitress wearing charming Normandy peasant costumes. (Bugni 2020)

Miss Olmsted described the Normandy Inn as a successful neighborhood project. Neighbors provided much of the food that was served, neighboring children served as waitresses, and the neighbor women brought their fruits to the inn, made their jams and jellies there, and sold them. At least 15 or 16 families cooperated in the project, and 14 farm girls earned enough money to go to college through their work at the inn. In the winter when the Inn was closed to the public, the community held their meetings there, and often gathered for square dances. ("Many Residents" 1940, 2)

Normandy Inn waitresses 1940; Barbara Martin, Imogene Maxudian,
Janis Teck, Lucille Stone, Mary Fenzel and Joan Doolittle
*Sodus Historical Society*

Donna D'Ercole Douglas recalls that "the two murals in the dinning wing were there when her father purchased the Normandy Inn years later" (D'Ercole 2023). Her father, Dom D'ercole, was the second owner of the Normandy Inn. Although there are no signatures on the murals, we suspect they were painted by Katherine Olmsted because of these clues; 1) Katherine had a three year college art degree, 2) the subjects in the murals appear to be French and 3) they are dancing, just like the local square dancers who used the new dining wing. One mural picture is located in the text here, and the other picture is on the back cover of the book, in color. The murals are beautifully painted and representative of happy times.

**Mural in Normandy in former dining hall, painted by Katherine Olmsted**

*Photo by Pamela Lee, taken courtesy of Terri Sanford and Erin Atkins, building owners*

# 4

## Adding A Gift Shop

Adding retail space is a smart move to bring extra sales to any business location and also provides additional interest for dinner guests. Many local wineries/tasting rooms in the Finger Lakes Wine Trails today have gift shops attached, which helps increase revenue. Katherine figured out the retail trick early on.

> Katie was always making changes and after the new dining room was added, around 1935, she re-modeled the upstairs dining balcony (formerly hay loft) into a gift shop and rural woman's exchange. Jenny Sergeant Contant operated the shop for many years, selling the homemade gifts brought in on consignment and several antiques of Katherine's. Freddy Sheppard was an all-around handy man at the Inn and took great pride in keeping everything dusted and cleaned for Jenny. Edna Olmsted later helped with the shop and also acted as receptionist when Katie needed her. (Wallington 1982, 79)

**Marjorie Contant, Country Store Manager**
*Sodus Historical Society*

"Katherine's 1943 menu invites guest to visit the Normandy Inn Peasant Bazaar on the second floor where there are gifts from many lands, antiques and American arts & crafts. The menu from 1943 (the 16th season) is very basic, printed on the front and back of a paper, then folded in half. Dinners were served every day with a choice of chicken, turkey, steak, duckling or trout for $1.50 and lunches served week days only for $1.00. No mention of the courses served" (*Normandy Inn Menu* 1943).

The Normandy Inn operating dates went through some changes over time. Upon first opening, the Inn was open year round for five years from 1927- 1931. According to *the Record*, "Recordings" (1931, 3), "the Inn would be closed for the first time during the winter months." Throughout various newspaper articles, it mentions closing for winter months anytime between November 1st and December 31st and reopening anywhere from March 31st – May 1st. The later years opening/closing dates found were on the Normandy Inn menu (1960), which states, "Normandy Inn is open April 1st – October 31st seven days a week from noon – 8 p.m."

Inserted here is a copy of the early Normandy Inn menu from 1943. Phot of the menu by Pamela Lee, courtesy of Rita Kilpatrick from her private collection.

## COME "WHEN IT'S APPLE BLOSSOM TIME IN NORMANDY"

NORMANDY INN is in the midst of large apple and cherry orchards - a real beauty spot "in Apple Blossom Time."  Also in "Lotus Blossom Time" - for in August, Egyptian lotus blossoms are in bloom nearby (this one of three places in the United States where lotus is to be found).

## COME FOR A WEEK-END OR FOR OVER NIGHT

Normandy Inn serves only meals - but will gladly arrange accommodations for guests : comfortable rooms in the neighborhood.

## FINE BATHING BEACH, Sodus Point, Lake Ontario

Clean Bath House facilities - ten minutes drive from the Inn - BOATING - FISHING

From *THE TRAVELER'S WINDFALL:*
"Where to Eat, Sleep and Play in the U.S.A."

NORMANDY INN: "Unique teahouse - charming atmosphere - many of the furnishings from Normandy - atmosphere doesn't get in the way of excellent and plentiful food and good service - cheese dishes - individual drip coffee."

French Cuisine

Normandy Inn Sodus

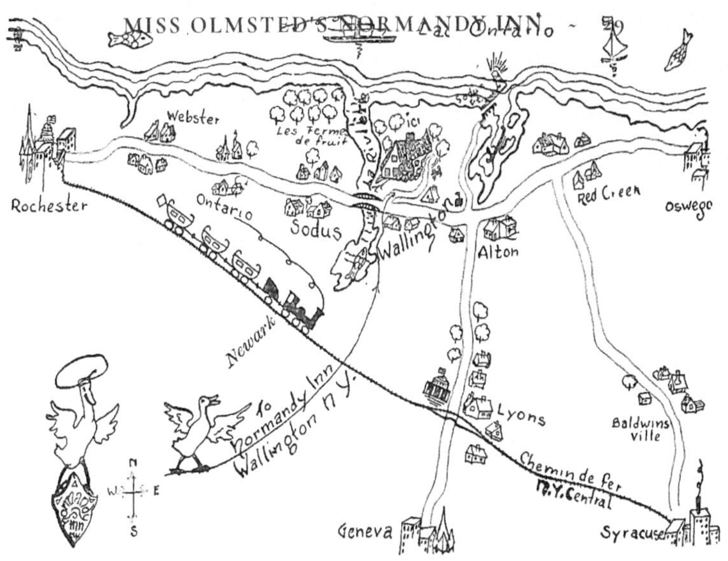


# Normandy Inn Sodus New York

Open for the 16th Season — April to November          Old World Atmosphere

Wayne County                    On Route 104                    2 Miles East of Sodus

Phone - Sodus 2497

## Katherine M. Olmsted - Proprietor

---

### SERVED EVERY DAY

Dinners - - - - 12 to 7:30 P. M. $1.50

*"The Dinner that made Normandy Inn Famous"*
Choice of chicken, turkey, steak, duckling, trout.

Child's Dinner — for children up to seven years - 75c

### SERVED WEEK DAYS ONLY

Luncheons - - - 12 to 2:30 P. M. $1.00

No Luncheons or teas served on Sundays or holidays.

SPECIAL PARTIES for Card Clubs - School Groups
Weddings - Receptions - Men's and Women's Organizations

---

### SERVED ON THURSDAY EVENING ONLY

"Maid's - Day - Out Special"

Continental Supper - - - - - $1.00

---

Visit The

NORMANDY INN PEASANT BAZAAR

Second Floor

Gifts from Many Lands - Antiques -
American Arts and Crafts

---

NORMANDY INN IS LISTED IN DUNCAN HINE'S "Adventures in Good Eating"

# 5

## The Great Depression

The Normandy Inn continued to do well throughout the beginnings of the Great Depression, as reported by Williams, with the addition of the dining room in 1932 and sales skyrocketing. However, the state of the economy would soon catch up to this sleepy town.

In the United States, the Great Depression began with the Wall Street Crash in October 1929 and then spread worldwide. The lowest point came in 1931-1933 and recovery came in 1940. The stock market crash marked the beginning of the decade of high unemployment, poverty, low profits, plunging farm income and lost opportunities for economic growth as well as personal advancement. (Encyclopedia Britannica, s.v. "The Great Depression," accessed August 8, 2023. *https://www.britannica.com/money* /topic/Great-Depression)

According to the History Channel, FDR Episode 1, "Nothing To Fear", the Great Depression was marked by high unemployment, business and bank failures, thousands of people in bread lines, people following vegetable trucks in the hopes that a cabbage would fall off, and people losing their homes, cars and being unable to feed their families. Immigrants were returning to their home countries. There was a mass feeling of hopelessness, the mood was of bleakness and despair and no hope that anything would get better.

FDR stepped up to the plate and studied what was causing the Great Depression. He hired a Brain Trust of experts, Economists, Teachers and Business people. They concurred that since the fall of Wall Street, the public had lost confidence and was no longer buying. They hid money in their mattresses. And because they weren't buying, there were no jobs. Factories were not hiring, businesses were laying off and farms failed. There were vast homeless encampments called "Hoovervilles". Unemployment was the problem, and the vicious cycle kept continuing. Food Banks had run out of donations, charities were bankrupt and at this time the government was not helping with any kinds of relief systems.

FDR began many new programs, Including the New Deal, WPA creating jobs, starting Social Security and many other programs. The economy started to recover in 1939, but it really took WWII to bring the economy out of the Great Depression. War is good for business, there were a lot of industry jobs making munitions, weapons, and planes for the armed forces. ("Nothing to Fear" 2023)

By 1936, the Normandy Inn was feeling the stress of customer's lower disposable income. According to correspondence in Katherine's Red Cross service file, "she learned of war bonuses for service rendered during WWI, and checked in with the local branch of the American Red Cross, Wayne County Chapter, in Newark, New York to apply for a war service bonus" (National Archives 1982 file 2 of 2, 56).

A letter in Katherine's Red Cross service file from Phoebe Murdock, Executive Secretary, to Mr. Don Smith, War Service

Department in Washington, D.C. on June 15, 1936 states in part, I have just been visited by Miss Katherine Olmsted of Wallington, N.Y., a former Red Cross nurse who saw active foreign war service. Miss Olmsted would like to know if she is eligible for the bonus and what the procedure would be for her to file application. ... she was sent to Russia and Roumania under Col. Anderson of Virginia who was in charge of that unit. She was active in foreign-service 1917-1918 and this particular unit remained a Red Cross one rather than being transferred to the army. She does not have an Adjusted Service Certificate. (National Archives 1982 file 2 of 2, 56)

A reply sent to Miss Phoebe Murdock from Ida Butler, Acting Director of Red Cross Nursing in Washington, D.C. on June 19, 1936 states in part, Miss Olmsted was never in war service with the Army or Navy. Her work in Europe was directly under the American Red Cross and later on in 1921 she became Director of Nursing in the League of Red Cross Societies. This means that she was never at any time federalized and did not serve directly with the Government during the period of the war, either in France or in this country, according to our records. (National Archives 1982 file 2 of 2, 53)

And so Katherine was not eligible for a war bonus for her Red Cross service during World War I. The bonus certainly would have helped during the Great Depression, but Katherine kept her tea shop going. And in doing so, provided much needed jobs for the local community. As reported in the Syracuse Post Standard years later, "Normandy Inn proved to a great asset to the rural community during the depression years, at one time supporting about 35 families. Enlarged again and again, Normandy Inn achieved an international reputation" (Miss Olmsted, 1964, 7).

Perhaps because of the Great Depression, "over the years, three of the Lent sisters returned to live in Wallington; Emma, Katherine's mother, and her aunts, Mary and Kathryn" (Wallington 1982, 70).

Following WWI, Miss Mary Lent quit the nursing profession and opened an antique shop in New York, in the Greenwich Village section. Following a successful business career, she decided to return to her old home in 1938, but was not content to retire entirely. She opened an antique shop in her home which she conducted until the time of her illness. Miss Mary Lent was widely traveled and had studied for a year in Germany and Italy. She had also traveled in the Far East. She was quite an authority on antiques and was deeply interested in history, probably being as well versed in the history of this section as anyone residing here. (Miss Mary Lent 1946, 1)

# 6

# World War II Impact

The local mail delivery during war time was intermittent, and described the Wallington Cobblestone Schoolhouse Restoration Committee.

> As the reputation of the Normandy Inn grew, so did its popularity for large banquets and dinner parties. Of course the party concerned always wrote or phoned ahead for reservations. The written requests for specific reservations sometimes arrived too late for the Inn to accommodate the party through no one's fault but the Wallington Post Office, which wasn't terribly efficient at the onset of World War II. This situation consequently forced Katherine to change post offices and from then on she received her mail through the Sodus Post Office, which seemed more efficient at the time. In fact the French food served at the Inn drew French people from Canada throughout New York State. (Wallington 1982, 72)

Rationing became common during the Second World War. Ration stamps were often used and these were redeemable for certain items.

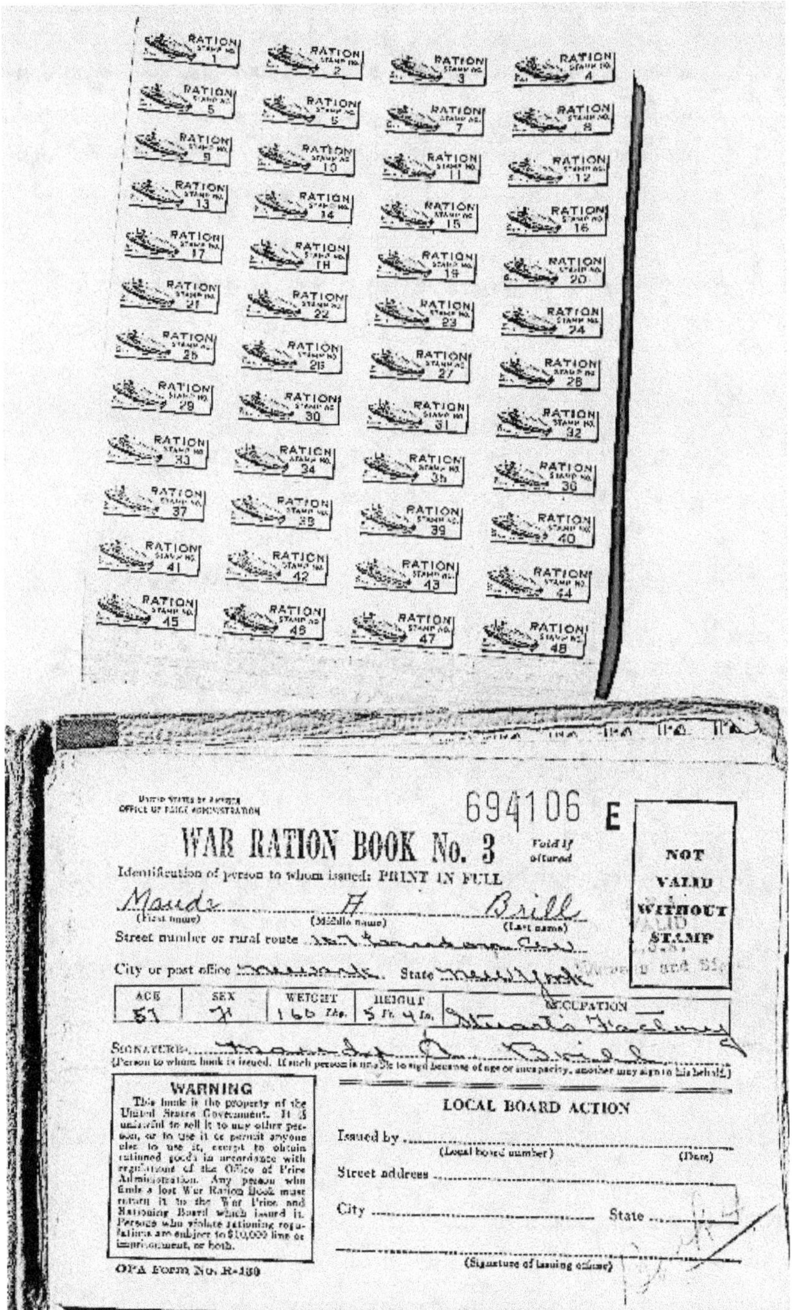

UNITED STATES OF AMERICA
OFFICE OF PRICE ADMINISTRATION

694106 E

# WAR RATION BOOK No. 3

Void if altered

NOT VALID WITHOUT STAMP

Identification of person to whom issued: PRINT IN FULL

Maude (First name) A (Middle name) Brill (Last name)

Street number or rural route

City or post office ... State ...

| AGE | SEX | WEIGHT | HEIGHT | OCCUPATION |
|---|---|---|---|---|
| 51 | F | 166 lbs. | 5 Ft. 4 In. | |

SIGNATURE ...
(Person to whom book is issued. If such person is unable to sign because of age or incapacity, another may sign in his behalf.)

**WARNING**

This book is the property of the United States Government. It is unlawful to sell it to any other person, or to use it or permit anyone else to use it, except to obtain rationed goods in accordance with regulations of the Office of Price Administration. Any person who finds a lost War Ration Book must return it to the War Price and Rationing Board which issued it. Persons who violate rationing regulations are subject to $10,000 fine or imprisonment, or both.

OPA Form No. R-130

**LOCAL BOARD ACTION**

Issued by ... (Local board number) (Date)

Street address ...

City ... State ...

... (Signature of issuing officer)

**World War II Ration Book**

*Maude A. Brill, author's great grandmother*

American civilians first received ration books—War Ration Book Number One, or the "Sugar Book"—on 4 May 1942, through more than 100,000 school teachers, Parent-Teacher Associations, and other volunteers. Sugar was the first consumer commodity rationed. Bakeries, ice cream makers, and other commercial users received rations of about 70% of normal usage. Coffee was rationed on 27 November 1942 to 1 pound every five weeks.

By the end of 1942, ration coupons were used for nine other items. Typewriters, gasoline, bicycles, footwear, silk, nylon, fuel oil, stoves, meat, lard, shortening and cooking oils, cheese, butter, margarine, processed foods (canned, bottled, and frozen), dried fruits, canned milk, firewood and coal, jams, jellies, and fruit butters were rationed by November 1943. (Bailey 1978, 110)

Even if you had the money, you were not able to purchase certain items if you did not have enough ration coupons. And then the stores may be out of stock on certain items, even if you had ration coupons. Restaurants and tea shops, like the Normandy Inn, were also rationed as they used pretty much all of these food items; sugar, coffee, meat, lard, cooking oils, margarine, fruit, milk, and possibly firewood and coal. My grandmother told me how difficult it was during the war time and how they made up new cooking recipes with food on hand. Her recipe for Wacky Chocolate Cake, made without eggs, was a staple during that time.

Gasoline rationing was also in force and this probably was also felt at the Normandy Inn, as folks wouldn't be able to travel to the Normandy Inn as frequently.

According to the social columns in the Syracuse Harold American quoted below, Katherine and her mother did not drive to Florida when the Inn closed for the winter in 1941. Instead they spent the winter with Katherine's uncle and cousin in Syracuse. Katherine's cousin, Anna, master minded a plan for Katherine to bring the Normandy Inn experience to the residents of Syracuse, and used her influence with friends and the museum. The plan unfolded in a news article published by the Syracuse Harold American, as quoted below.

Miss Katherine Olmsted is passing the winter with her uncle, Will H. Olmsted and cousin, Miss Anna W. Olmsted, Director of the museum, at their home in James Street. Last Sunday Miss Anna W. Olmsted gave a tea for her aunt, Mrs. A.L. Olmsted and her daughter, Miss Katherine. There were a score or so of guests-close friends of the hostess. Presiding at the tea table which was centered with daffodils, were Miss Ethel Mundy, noted miniature painter, and Mrs. Washington Platt.

Katherine Olmsted Announced Favored Recipes of Famous People at Museum Class. Tomorrow's lesson in "Good Eating in America" , Miss Katherine Olmsted's cooking course in the Syracuse Museum's Living Kitchen, will bring to attention favorite recipes of famous people. There will be such good things favored by Lawrence Tibbett, Clark Gable, the Duchess of Windsor, Oscar of the Waldorf and Antoine of New Orleans. Tuesday's course on "Eating 'Round the World" will feature fish dishes. Miss Olmsted patterns menus with an eye on the budget. (E.V.W. 1942, 13)

Katherine conducted many cooking courses, consisting of six lessons for $10, in Syracuse at the museum from January – February 1942. Some of these included Pennsylvania Dutch recipes with museum members bringing pottery to show how a table was set in the early Pennsylvania Dutch days, and she repeated the cooking classes "Romance of Eating 'Round the World" due to its popularity. Good Eating in America – had an emphasis on economy and present day nutritional requirements. Favorite Recipes of Famous People, which must have been a big hit as it was also repeated. Each lesson offered a complete meal to be eaten by the class. (Series of Cooking Lessons 1942, 13)

Cousin Anna kept Katherine busy, as noted in the Syracuse Museum of Fine Arts Quarterly Bulletin for Jan – Mar 1942, (7) "Katherine is advertised as part of a Red Cross Nutrition-Canteen Course in World's Fair Kitchen of Syracuse Museum. She also had a featured article, which summarized her WWI amazing adventure and provided her picture in Red Cross uniform."

In April that year, Katherine closed the Normandy Inn from 1942-1944 during World War II. In a letter to the Red Cross HQ September 8, 1942, Katherine states, "These days of war and distress give me a real longlining to get back into some Red Cross Service again. I am forced to close my Normandy Inn because of gasoline rationing. I have been teaching Red Cross Home Nursing and Canteen classes and have taken a refresher course to be on our Community Nursing Squad (National Archives 1978, file 2 of 2, 73-74)." "In 1942 Katherine offered to travel to Washington for an interview if the Red Cross was interested. She recognized her age could be working against her and mentioned this in the letter, Katherine was 54 at this time. Enclosed with the letter is a copy the Normandy Inn menu for the coming 16th season, which did not occur. Also enclosed is a resume of Katherine's work experience (National Archives 1978, file 2 of 2, 66, 68-69, 73-74)." The work situation must have been desperate for Katherine to consider appealing to the Red Cross for work, recalling her strong resignation letter to the League of Red Cross Societies sixteen years earlier.

Toward the end of 1942, Emma Olmsted, Katherine's mother, became very ill and passed away on February 1, 1943. The local newspaper, The Record, provided detailed information:

MRS. EMMA OLMSTED SUCCUMBS TO ILLNESS Mrs. Emma Olmsted passed away this morning at the home of her sister, Miss Kathryn Lent, following a long illness. Funeral arrangements which had not been made at the time The Record went to press will be in charge of the H S Norton Co. Mrs. Olmsted was well known in this community and was also well acquainted with many persons from long distances who had dined at Normandy Inn at Wallington, operated by her daughter Miss Katherine Olmsted who is now in Syracuse. Besides the daughter and sister mentioned, Mrs. Olmsted is survived by a son Harry of Rochester and another sister, Miss Mary Lent of Wallington. (Mrs. Emma Olmsted 1943, 1)

"Katherine remained with her cousin Anna in Syracuse for a few years, per her annual Red Cross survey" (National Archives 1978, file 2 of 2, 58-65). "The Normandy Inn continued to be closed in 1943 and Katherine gave lectures on Home and Farm Safety. She also gave lectures on the prevention of accidents in the home and on the farm, at a meeting of the State Home and Farm Safety Advisory Committee. Katherine was a field representative of the Office of Civilian Mobilization of the State War Council" (Prevention of Accidents 1943).

"After no response from the Red Cross employment inquiry, mailed on Sep 8, 1942, Kathrine mailed a second request to Red Cross HQ a year and a half later March 1, 1944 and included an updated resume" (National Archives 1978, file 2 of 2, 46). The Director of Nursing, Washington, D.C. finally replied on April 4, 1944 and stated, "At present, the Red Cross is not sending nurses overseas. We have referred a good many applicants to UNRA. The American Red Cross is not doing any independent nursing work in Europe other than that which Harvard Red Cross nurses are carrying on. I will not forget your interest and we will keep your address safely on file" (National Archives 1978 file 2 of 2, 45).

Although Katherine received a decline letter from the Red Cross, she persevered and continued speaking engagements over these couple of years. According to a survey of various newspaper announcements, "she provided speeches for the Canteen Red Cross (National Archives 1978, file 2 of 2, 76-77), Safety at Home and on the Farm (Miss Olmsted to Speak, 1945) and talks on her experience during WWI in Europe as a nurse, according to the Geneva Daily Times" (1944, 7). And many more not listed here. A local reporter remembers Katherine fondly in the following quote.

> Gifted with a quick intelligence, a great fund of human sympathy and understanding, practical common sense and a magnetic personal charm that opened many tightly closed doors, she was an immediate success in the then very new field of public health nursing. Once she spoke in Futon on a Red Cross fund drive and I have never forgotten her striking appearance and her eloquence in pleading the Red Cross cause (Lynch 1968).

**Katherine Olmsted showing antiques**
*Picture courtesy of Rita Kilpatrick, private collection*

"A creative cooking article was published in the New York Herald Tribune June 17, 1945 titled, "That Cordon Bleu Touch" submitted by Katherine Olmsted. Katherine provided some recipes and offered additional recipes of French Desserts for sale by coupon order (Olmsted K. 1945)." By the time 1945 rolled around, Katherine sold recipes rather than provided cooking classes, as previously in 1942. "That Cordon Bleu Touch" newspaper article is copyrighted and therefore is not available for print. Have no worries though, there is a chapter on French recipes coming up in this book, keep reading!

# 7

## Winters in New York

To add insult to injury while the Normandy Inn was closed, the winter of February 1945 proved to have a very heavy snow. An article in the local Record newspaper provided a good description of the damage and how the community came together to help out. And this was not surprising considering that the Normandy Inn was thought of as the place to meet and was widely used by local residents.

Normandy Inn at Wallington will be open this spring in spite of the thousands of dollars-worth of damage entailed when the roof caved in because of heavy snow last week. Miss Katherine Olmsted was home last Friday and made arrangements to have the work of reconstruction started Monday morning.

The roof over the large dining room will have to be removed in its entirety and the bulging walls will have to be reinforced, with much new material replacing broken parts.

The roof caved into the second floor, but fortunately, most of the articles on that floor had been removed and the tables there had served to stop the roof from falling farther.

This new part of the inn was built several years ago. It

housed a downstairs dining room and an upstairs one that was used for overflow guests when the inn was busy.

Wallington firemen and women of the Wallington community removed a large part of the furnishings, dishes and items from the lower floor after the roof began to sag in, in order to prevent further damage.

April 1ˢᵗ had been the date set for the opening, but this may have to be delayed a short time. (Inn to be Reopened 1945, 1)

And through adversity came opportunity. The Syracuse Herald American reported, "when the roof caved in 1945 due to heavy snow, there was more remodeling to allow an open space above the center of the dining hall proper" (VanWormer 1947). The pictures of the Normandy Inn building over time show improvements, which supports this statement.

"Each spring before the reopening, Miss Olmsted invited the entire staff to her home, known as the Big House, and she cooked dinner for them before they discussed business and changes for the year" (Wallington 1982, 78). The group of returning staff had a lot to discuss in 1945, after a two year closure during war time and then a huge repair after snow damage.

# 8

# Emerging Renewed

The prior news article regarding the very heavy snow indicated that the Inn was slated to reopen in April 1945. It was after these challenging experiences of the Great Depression and WWII that "Katherine listed her business interest as "My Own Restaurant" instead of a "tea shop", per her annual Red Cross Survey"(National Archives 1978, file 2 of 2, 58). With relief in sight, another boon occurred when "all rationing in the United States ended in 1946 according to Bailey" (1978, 117), and this was a burden lifted off of many businesses.

Katherine forged ahead with new plans when the Inn reopened in 1945. Photos show an enchanting entrance to the Inn with beautiful landscaping, newly designed peasant dresses for the waitresses, "a renewed vigor for the renamed Country Store, previously called the Peasant Bazaar and a seriously updated menu made with sturdy cardboard and multiple French courses with food descriptions" (Normandy Inn Menu 1960). "It was after the years of hardship that public interest renewed in the restaurant and many famous people visited the Normandy Inn. Word of the Normandy Inn spread far and wide based on information in the scrapbook and autograph books. This notoriety helped grow the customer base for Katherine" (Kilpatrick 2023).

Main entrance to the Normandy Inn circa 1950, showing the
expansive gardens and remodeling features, including the north
dining room to the left

The cover of this book is Katherine's 1960 menu design front, photograph granted by Donna D'Ercole Douglas. It is of the French Flag with large stripes of blue, white and red. Located at the top is a French Fleur-de-Lis style design.

The menu back, pictured below, includes a sketched map with directions to the Normandy Inn and a goose, reminiscent of those that flocked the original Inn. The unique sketches add a personal flair to the menu design. Once again, we suspect that Katherine Olmsted designed the menu and drew the map, based on her background in art and fondness of her business.

The map below appeared in the 1960 Normandy Inn menu. The 1960 Normandy Inn Menu states "Opens under the same management, Katherine Olmsted, for its 33rd season".

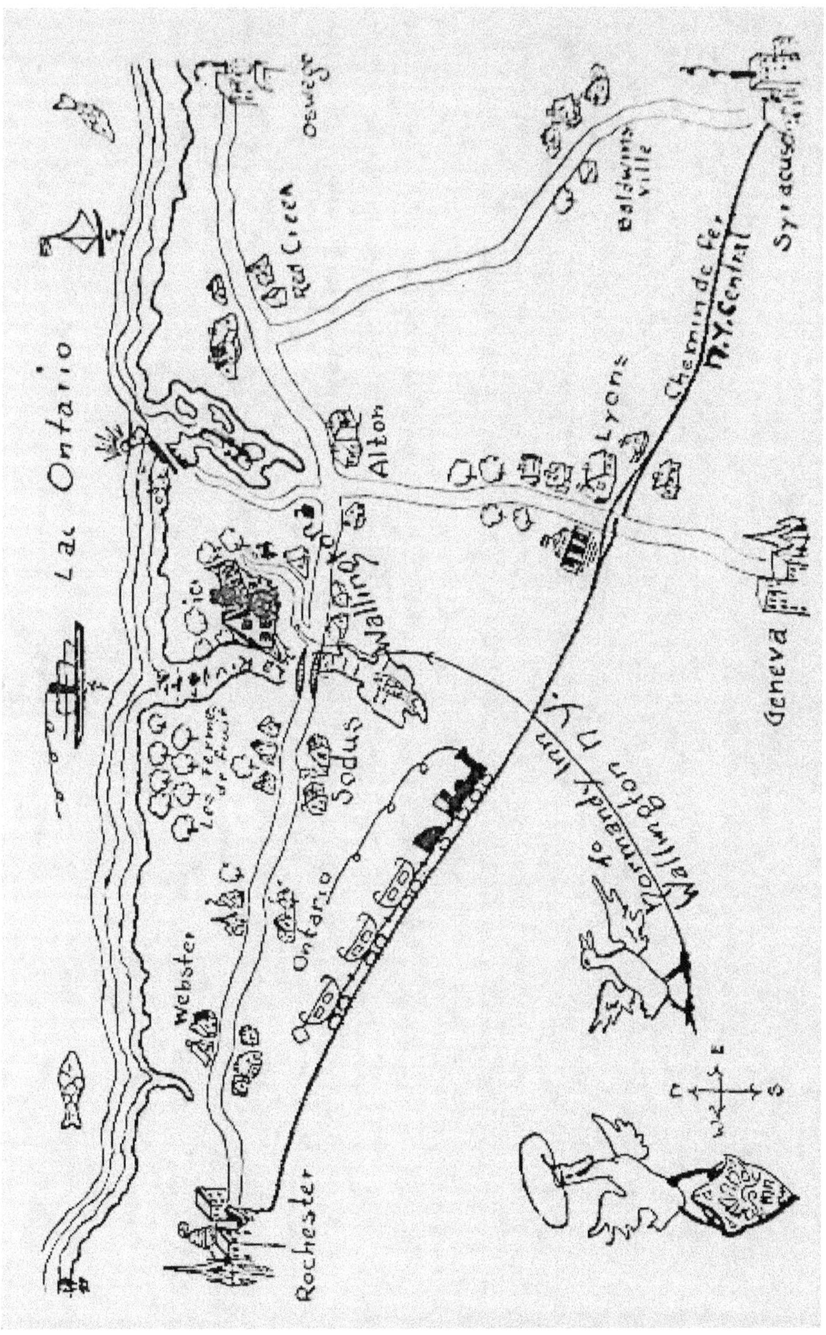


**1960 Normandy Inn Menu back**
*Photograph by Pamela Lee, Donna D'Ercole Douglas private collection*

NORMANDY INN has a quiet charm which provides an ideal atmosphere for leisurely dining. The discerning, often tired traveler, and those who seek a new and delightful place will enjoy entertaining visiting friends and relatives, or celebrating some special occasion such as a birthday or anniversary at famous Normandy Inn.

Many of our patrons have made a practise of following the season changes at our Inn in its attractive rural setting. In the midst of large apple and cherry orchards, here is a real beauty spot - "In Apple Blossom Time", again when the lilacs are in bloom, and when the brilliant colors of autumn tint the countryside.

ATMOSPHERE. Patterned after the rural Inns in the Province of Normandy, France, where its owner manager lived for many years, an atmosphere of gayety and peace, and the service which comes from a deep feeling of hospitality.

NORMANDY INN opens for the season every year on April 1, and closes on October 31. It is open every day of the week from 12 noon to 8 P.M.

The Inn has two dining rooms - the larger seating about 200 and the smaller about 40.

SPECIAL PARTIES, special parties are welcome, whether they number ten or 200. They are given the continuous personal attention of the manager and her assistants. Arrangements for these must be made in advance.

CUISINE The cuisine, based on French cooking, includes such Normandy Inn specialties as French Onion Soup, Coquille St. Jacque, and individual French drip coffee. Wines, from the finest New York State Vintages, may be ordered separately by those who enjoy a special wine for a special occasion. Cocktails and Mixed Drinks are served at the tables or in the Cocktail Lounge.

COUNTRY STORE The Inn's latest addition for the interest of its guests is the Country Store, where handicraft of many kinds and different values may be purchased, and where men and women who take pride in the skill of their hands may display their products to the Inn's discriminating guests.

LOCATION Easily reached from a radius of more than a hundred miles, the Inn is located in the heart of Wayne County, among its charming rolling hills and close to Lake Ontario's beautiful beaches. State Highway 104 runs right past its entrance. Altho Normandy Inn has only a few overnight rooms for guests, we will gladly arrange for accomodations nearby, whether for a night or a week.

CALL SODUS 3244 or write for information or reservations for parties of over 10. Reservations are not necessary for smaller parties.

NORMANDY INN opens at Sodus, New York this spring for its 27th season under the same management of its owner Katherine Olmsted.

**1960 Normandy Inn Menu back**

*Photograph by Pamela Lee, Donna D'Ercole Douglas private collection*

# - Luncheons -

Served daily 12 noon to 2:30 P. M.
- Not on Sundays or Holidays -

Entrees with Potatoes - Vegetables - Rolls
Relishes - Beverage

Chicken Breast Normandy .......... $1.50
Pork Chop - Applesauce ............ $1.50
Creamed Chicken - Patty Shell ... $1.50
Omelet
    Plain - Jelly - Ham - Cheese . $1.50
Fish du Jour ........................... $1.50
Griddle Cakes - Sausage ............. $1.25
Chicken Chow Mein .................... $1.50
Small Sirloin Steak .................... $1.60
Lamb Chop (1) .......................... $1.60

# Desserts - See Menu

# - Salad Plate -

Shrimp ........................................ $1.65
Turkey - Fruit - Chicken - Ham .. $1.50

# - Sandwiches -

Egg - Ham - Cheese - Chicken ..... $1.00

*Todays Special*

**1960 Normandy Inn Menu**
*Photograph by Pamela Lee, Donna D'Ercole Douglas private collection*

# NORMANDY INN DINNER

## Served Daily - 12 noon to 8 P.M.

## INCLUDES

| | |
|---|---|
| *Les Hors d'Oeuvres* | Fruit Cup Supreme .......................................... |
| | Tomato or Grapefruit Juice ............................... |
| | Chilled Fruit Juice Frappe ............................... |
| | Jumbo Shrimp Cocktail .................... 60¢ Extra |
| | |
| *Les Potages* | Soup à l'oignon Gratinée ................................ |
| | Le Consommé au Sherry ................................ |
| | Homemade Vegetable Soup ........................... |
| | |
| *Les Poissons* | Le Coquille St Jacques ................................. |
| | |
| *Entrées* | Roast Turkey - Cranberry Sauce ............ 2 ᵒᵒ |
| | Roast Young Duckling ..................... 3 ᵒᵒ |
| | Chicken a la' Normandy ................... 2 50 |
| | Fish - Lake or Brook Trout .............. 2 ᵒᵒ |
| | Baked Ham - Sauce du Vin ............... 2 85 |
| | Pork Chops (2) Applesauce ............. 2 85 |
| | Lamb Chops (2) Mint Jelly .............. 3 ᵒᵒ |
| | Fried Jumbo Shrimp ...................... 3 25 |
| | Chicken Breast Sauté ..................... 3 00 |
| | Half Young Broiler Sauté ............... 3 ᵒᵒ |
| | Fried Scallops ............................. 2 50 |
| | Large Choice Porterhouse Steak ........ 3.9 ᵒ |
| | |
| *Salade* | Salade à la Francaise .................................. |
| | |
| *Desserts* | See Special Menu ..................................... |
| | |
| *Café* | Coffee - Tea - Sanka - Milk ........................ |

| | |
|---|---|
| *Aujourdui nous Recommandons* | Planked Tenderloin Steak 3 50 |

1960 Normandy Inn Menu

*Photograph by Pamela Lee, Donna D'Ercole Douglas private collection*

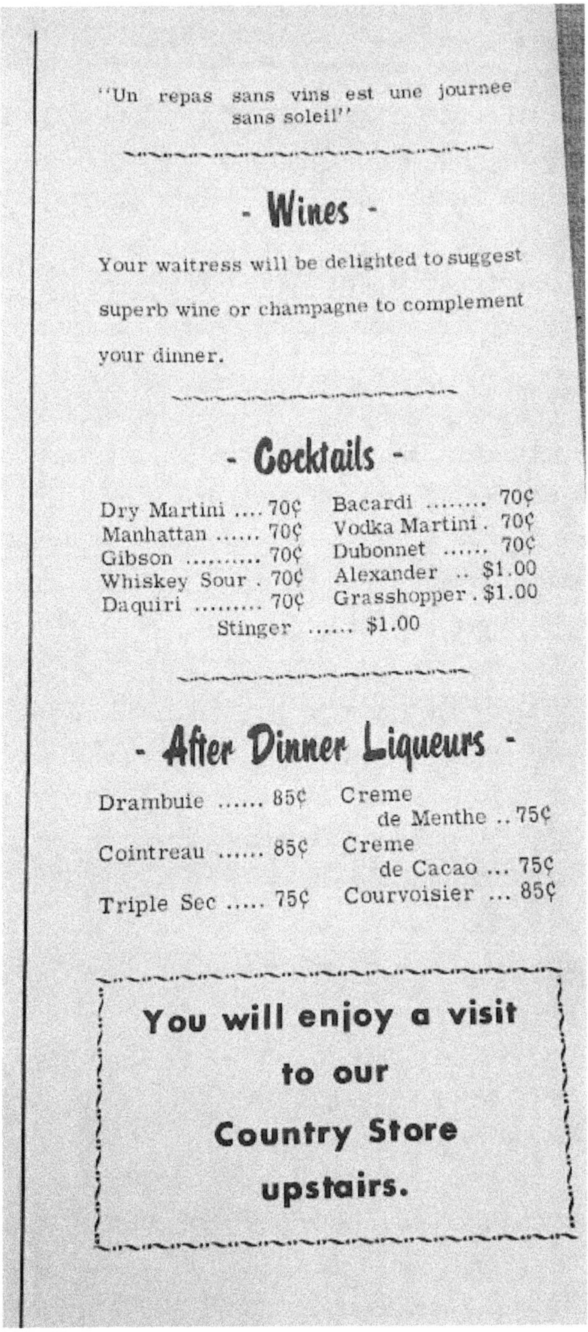

"Un repas sans vins est une journee
sans soleil"

## - Wines -

Your waitress will be delighted to suggest

superb wine or champagne to complement

your dinner.

## - Cocktails -

| | | | |
|---|---|---|---|
| Dry Martini .... 70¢ | Bacardi ........ 70¢ |
| Manhattan ...... 70¢ | Vodka Martini . 70¢ |
| Gibson .......... 70¢ | Dubonnet ...... 70¢ |
| Whiskey Sour . 70¢ | Alexander .. $1.00 |
| Daquiri ......... 70¢ | Grasshopper . $1.00 |

Stinger ...... $1.00

## - After Dinner Liqueurs -

| | |
|---|---|
| Drambuie ...... 85¢ | Creme de Menthe .. 75¢ |
| Cointreau ...... 85¢ | Creme de Cacao ... 75¢ |
| Triple Sec ..... 75¢ | Courvoisier ... 85¢ |

## You will enjoy a visit
## to our
## Country Store
## upstairs.

**1960 Normandy Inn Menu**

*Photograph by Pamela Lee, Donna D'Ercole Douglas private collection*

"Prices calculated in 2023 dollars compared to 1960 amount of $3.00 is $30.49 for a dinner" (Webster, 2023). "The meal includes a glass of wine, soup, le coquille St. Jacques, entrée, salad, rolls, dessert and beverage" (Normandy Inn Menu, 1960).

Roy Hawks, a Syracuse Herald Food Critic, did a great job of describing the Normandy Inn menu and atmosphere in 1963. He also provided directions from Syracuse.

A delightful spring drive in the midst of blooming apple and cherry orchards brings you to famous Normandy Inn on Route 104, near Sodus, New York. The owner-proprietor Katherine Olmsted returned from Florida last month to re-open her inn for its 36th season – open every day from 12 o'clock noon to 8 p.m. until October 31.

The menu reads like a gourmet's delight. Besides a wide variety of cocktails, to be ordered from the menu, a choice of a free glass of red or white wine is offered by attractive young waitresses in Normandy peasant costumes; of special appeal to diners who like wine with their meals in the European fashion. And if you know France, you will realize that Normandy Inn seems to transport you to a bit of the French countryside in the heart of rural America.

Of course there are many good restaurants with pleasing décor, but those in-the-know agree that here is something "just a little different"-something unique among places to dine. A simple rustic building has been made over from a century old barn, its hand-hewn timbers resulting in perfect acoustics, with quiet assured even when the rooms are crowded.

The charming atmosphere is enhanced by soft lighting, partially by candlelight; by antique French Provincial furniture and by the owner's rare collection of copper, brass and pewter utensils obtained from ancient Normandy kitchens in France; a collection so noteworthy that it has been shown in its entirety in the Rochester Museum of Arts and Sciences.

But more important than its atmosphere to lovers of good food, are the specialties of the Inn, including French onion soup, Coquille St. Jacques, Duck supreme and coffee served in individual coffee filters imported from France.

Music is provided by Alice Lee Bourne, one of America's outstanding harpists, who has played in several states along the east coast. This is no ordinary dinner music, for Miss Bourne's repertoire of classical and semi-classical pieces, exquisitely played is delightful. (Hawks 1963, 24)

Dining "eatertainment" is a newly coined phrase, however, this description aptly fits the Normandy Inn. Many people may not travel to France, but a short excursion to the Normandy Inn, Sodus New York, would immerse diners in the tastes, scenery and sounds of the French provincial countryside.

# 9

Atmosphere at
Normandy Inn

Many improvements were seen, based on the updated front entrance picture in the previous chapter. The Normandy Inn looked like a Tudor castle after the updates. The best description of the building appearance from the 1950s was located in the Arms' Crossroads-Wallington book, written and published by local residents. Below is an excerpt.

> The grounds were once a botanical paradise, filled with lovely flowering trees. Lotus grew in the pond which has now been filled in. Violets grew profusely in the small woods and banks that framed the front of the Inn, and pink and white dogwood bloomed all around. Every table was graced with flower arrangements from the grounds surrounding this nationally known inn. Pauline Caroltta Baker, a waitress at that time, remembers picking peppermint from the creek shores, to be used in fresh salads and as garnishes. (Wallington 1982, 79)

**Normandy Inn sketch by Frijs Babcock featured on a post card**
*Gift from Chris Davis, Historian*

The atmosphere was also filled with unique sounds. Here is a quirky tale about a background sound at the Inn.

> With the perfection Miss Olmsted had about her Inn, the porch door remained squeaky for years. Why? Many pondered and even offered their assistance, but were always put off with one excuse or another. Finally she revealed that it was an easy way of noting people's "comings and goings", since the money was kept at the receptionist's desk just inside the door. Sly as a fox she was! (Wallington 1982, 79-80)

Of course, there were beautiful background sounds at the Inn as well, much better than squeaky doors. The orchestra and harp music added to an elegant dining experience.

One time students from the Eastman School of Music in Rochester, New York, asked Katherine if she needed an orchestra. Her reply was that of course she did. She arranged for the boys to sleep in the attic on the weekends and naturally fed them all they could eat.

Later the music at Normandy Inn was regularly furnished by Alice Lee Bourne of Lyons, New York. An accomplished harpist, Miss Bourne's music most people remember and returned to hear again and again. She remained at the Normandy Inn through the 1963 season. (Wallington 1982, 75)

**Alice Lee Bourne with harps**
*Rita Kilpatrick*

Rita Kilpatrick provided a picture of Alice Bourne during her interview. "A former diner of the Normandy told me that Alice Bourne, harpist, sat in a corner of the dining room and on busy occasions like Easter or Mother's Day, would sit upstairs and the harp music would waft down over the balcony" (unknown 2023).

# IO

# The People of Normandy Inn

The best descriptions of the staff and customers were provided by that same source, the Arms' Crossroads-Wallington. It is astonishing that so much was remembered in 1982 about the Inn thirty years before. Here are some choice remembrances.

> There were a series of chefs at Normandy Inn, each staying a few years. Fernand was the first chef brought over from France by Katherine. He was a student and after two years left for New York City to pursue his studies to become a doctor. Joseph Pierre Hertzfeld followed from Vienna. Katherine Olmsted presented Pierre as Executive Manager of the Normandy Inn and Viennese Coffee Lounge. For whatever reason, this arrangement did not work out and he left the Normandy Inn to open the Old World Inn in Newark around 1945. (Wallington 1982, 78)

Hertzfeld's departure prior to 1945 coincided with the Inn's closure during WWII. Below is his business card, thought to have been designed by Katherine Olmsted.

57

JOSEPH PIERRE HERTZFELD
*Executive Manager*

NORMANDY INN AND
VIENNESE COFFEE LOUNGE

SODUS, NEW YORK

## ABOUT
## *PIERRE*

Pierre is Operating Manager of this famous French Restaurant. He has a wealth of experience from abroad having worked in or managed exclusive establishments such as Fauchon in Paris, Huyler's in New York City, Tacosi in Rome, Gourmand in Budapest, Peschta in Vienna and many others.

Pierre is an expert French pastry chef and cook.

Pierre is also an accomplished musician and former violin soloist in his own concerts in Vienna, Austria. He organized the Wayne County Concert Orchestra and is it's present Conductor, entertaining his guests at the piano or violin on many occasions.

**Pierre Hertzfeld Business Card circa 1940**
*Edson Ennis, Historian, private collection*

For historic accounts of other staff of the Normandy Inn, the Arms' Crossroads-Wallington volunteers gathered quite a bit of information.

There were several chefs in the interim before Ethel Messinger took over. Ethel's homemade rolls were the best ever tasted in these parts. Dorothy Norris was soon hired during this time and trained under Ethel. She took over as head chef when Ethel retired, and continued to run the kitchen for 30 years afterward. Dorothy remembers her interview when she was scared and had to admit that at 32 years old she had never worked before. Miss Olmsted just smiled and said, "Good, we'll teach you our way."

The bungalow which Miss Olmsted and her mother originally lived in was used to house refugees after Work War II. One couple from Lithuania, Olga and Janas Bosenbaughm, remained with their two girls to help with the Inn for several years. Janas was the bookkeeper and helped take care of the grounds while Olga was noted for her delicious petit-fours. They lived in the bungalow, but the entire family ate all meals in the Inn.

Hobos were a good source of short-term, capable help for Katie and she always had a good meal ready. Dorothy Norris remembers a tall, thin gentleman with a wrapped bag on a stick who came to the door one evening. Katherine instructed her to "fix up the best turkey dinner we have". After partaking the feast, the hobo asked what chore he could do as payment. Miss Olmsted explained that she had nothing urgent and was just glad he enjoyed the dinner. The hobo insisted he must pay something and pulled from his bundle a pair of wooden shoes that hung for many years on the parlor mantel. (Wallington 1982, 78-81)

And the customers were just as interesting as the staff. According to local interviews by the same source,

> On the guest list there seemed to be an unusual number of doctors from as far away as New York City, which could have been attributed to Katherine's connection with the Red Cross.
>
> Normandy always drew a crowd on holidays with over 500 dinners, along with being a favorite spot for influential Rochester and Syracuse natives any weekend. This included older widows in their limousines, so there was a special table set aside just for their chauffeurs. (Wallington 1978, 80)

Many of these society ladies from Syracuse may have been introduced to Katherine at the tea her cousin hosted during the Inn's closure, in 1942. Some of the ladies may have even attended the cooking classes at the Syracuse Museum's Living Kitchen a few years earlier. "Rita Kilpatrick showed me the 1958 autograph book maintained by the Inn. Some of the famous people attending dinner in 1958 were Dwight D. Eisenhower, Willie Mays, Mickey Mantel and Jayne Mansfield" (Kilpatrick 2023).

And of course, the most interesting person was Katherine herself. Her kindness to the Wallington residents, refugees and hobos is impressive. And on the other end of the spectrum, Katherine entertained the well-to-do celebrities and doctors. Lynch sums up Katherine's personality very well in this short quote.

> Katherine Olmsted was always the same, whether she was standing by Herbert Hoover as they received a specially designed medal of thanks for their help to Belgium from King Albert of the Belgians or discussing with a farm neighbor the best way to preserve fruit – a truly great woman whose love of humanity never faltered (Lynch 1968).

Katherine Olmsted, center, surrounded by Normandy Inn waitresses
circa 1935
*Sodus Historical Society*

**I I**

# The Business Woman

Katherine was a progressive business woman and ahead of her time, when many women did not have careers outside the home. There are many news articles about her business related talks given at various meetings. Some of her more interesting quotes include,

> "Imagination means business" began a speech by Miss Katherine Olmsted. She has built up at $100,000 yearly business from an original investment of $163. "Can't I do it a little better or a little different?" is the imaginative approach to selling something you make or do, Miss Olmsted said. (Davis 1948, 29)

Katherine also was featured in an article regarding her Country Store concept. She reportedly had "guests attend from 30 New York area towns and cities and even one attendee from New Hampshire" (Country Store Excites, Jul 8, 1948).

> Also attending were representatives from the New York State Department of Commerce. This group's goal was to help men and women increase business skills and the tea she hosted brought this group together.

According to the article, demonstrations were provided by craftswomen who made silver jewelry, woven articles and painted tin ware. The Normandy Inn Country Store had craft items from approximately 70 persons. (Country Store Excites 1948, 1)

The following 1950 Post Standard article described Katherine's interest in hand crafted items and how she helped people turn their hobbies into income. There is a description of the wide variety of items in this article.

Some of the items in "former hay loft" shopping center include shirttail aprons, mugs made from discarded beer bottles, hand crafted incense burners, handmade hooked and crocheted rugs, ceramics, neckties, dusting mitts, sea shell jewelry, dressed dolls, birds made from pine cones, and homemade jams and jellies.

One of the consignees, a young engineer who developed several differed items in metal, turned his hobby into a profitable business. He has made some stunning copper ash trays and candle holders.

Miss Olmsted believes in using the things at hand. A piece of driftwood with interesting contour had been polished and varnished and its beauty compared with modern art at its best.

When it comes to her own hobby, Miss Olmsted has picked the "C's" – cooking and collecting. Unusual dishes have always intrigued her and during the years that she was in France with the International Red Cross, she sought the out-of-way restaurants, each with its own special dish. And so she collected the recipes. Then she had to have something to cook them in, so she began collecting kettles, pans, pots, bowls, bottles and all sorts of interesting utensils. Miss Olmsted has a rare old Gothic pine bread chest which is 300 years old and has been converted into her desk. (A.F.K. 1950, 17)

Katherine spoke at various engagements on business related topics. "At a State Commerce Dinner she provided an excellent quote about her recipe for success. First of all, you've got to enjoy what you're doing. Otherwise, don't bother. You have to have perseverance. Above all you need a sense of humor." (Women Support 1950, 20).

And the Buffalo Courier-Express newspaper briefly quoted the body of that same speech.

> Katherine Olmsted advised more than 300 women at the dinner clinic that valuable help for novice business women is available from friendly neighbors and community residents. In repayment, she added, the first thing to remember is what you can do for the community. As an example, she related that in the early history of Normandy Inn, neighbors took home chickens to roast for the inn. Now, every other week a community barn dance is held at the Inn and the dining hall is used for community meetings.
>
> Women who want to have fun and aren't afraid to work hard can establish business on a shoestring. In contrast to the practice of men who believe they must have a large capital to begin a business, we women aren't afraid to start on a shoestring. When I first started the restaurant, I didn't have anything to lose. So I didn't worry. The chief reason for women setting up shop for themselves ought to be to have a lot of fun and have a happy time. To succeed without capital, however, will mean hard work in the beginning-as long as 15 or 18 hours a day. (Marjorie 1950, 14)

Women first received to right to vote during Katherine's lifetime. "Women's Right to Vote was received in Finland 1906, United Kingdom and Germany 1918, Austria and Netherlands 1919 and United States

1920 (Encyclopedia Britannica, s.v. "Women's Suffrage," accessed August 8, 2023, https://www.britannica.com/topic/woman-suffrage)." Katherine's speech in today's gender neutral sensitivity may seem a bit pointed comparing men to women, however the 1950s was an era where women had begun asserting themselves after years of political oppression and appears to be in-line with thinking of that time.

**Katherine with Macie, her faithful friend and companion, 1956**
*Old Internationals Newsletter, October 1956*

Katherine's business sense served her well and the business growth is commented upon in later years, as summarized in the news articles below.

The little Country Store grew over the years and in 1961 served as a rural Women's Exchange for over 100 consignees from all the state. Located on the second floor of the building, the Country Store offers beautiful needlework and hand-made articles. (Elwood 1960)

And in 1963, Hawks tells readers that they want to make sure to see Country Store on the second floor of the Inn. He stated that the wares included beautiful needlework and hand-made consignment items made by artisans in many locations throughout New York State. He also pointed out that Katherine's enterprise provided advice in packaging, presentation and pricing to consignment artisans. The Country Store was a wonderful opportunity for artisans to turn their skills and hobbies into income. (Hawks 1963, 24)

# 12

# Supporting the Youth

Katherine truly cared for the community she lived in, especially the youth. The very best descriptions of her community involvement came directly from those same residents thirty years later. The Wallington Cobblestone Schoolhouse Restoration Committee gathered these memories for the book they published in 1982.

Over the years, Katherine's favorite groups to use the Inn were the French classes from many area high schools and colleges. The French classes were treated to French menus, especially designed by Katie, French food and a talk in French, given by Katie after dinner.

Katherine, who never married nor had children of her own, was particularly fond of young people and hired many young girls to work in the Inn during the summer months. The majority of these girls were working to earn money for college and some were the daughters of local farmers. Some sixty-percent of the area girls earned their education from working at the Normandy. Besides hiring them for the summer, during the 1930's many roomed in a dormitory built at the back of her grandfather's home, by her aunt Mary. Later, Mary used this Studio Room as an antique shop.

The owner-proprietor grew very close to her employees as they did to her. One could imagine the astonishment when she found that the girls had marked up the ladies' room by scribbling their names on the lavatory. She had every intention of punishing the waitresses, but upon further investigation, she came to the inscription "We have the best boss in the world." And naturally all was quickly forgiven.

Most people who worked for Katherine for any length of time remember her as a perfectionist, influenced by no one, and tolerating no diversifying from routine, with the "customer being right-no matter what". But underneath all this was a caring "mother" to whom the girls could turn to with any problem.

Don and Lois Fisher have many memories of their days at the Normandy. Lois was hired as a water girl in 1949 for Easter Sunday and was personally taught by Katherine to be a waitress, as were all the girls. She worked at the Normandy Inn 14 years. Miss Olmsted treated them to a wedding dinner for 12 and Miss Alice Lee Bourne played the harp. Don and Lois were soon gifted with son Douglas and a few years later were trying for a second child. A trip to Dr. Munzner diagnosed that both she and Don were "trying too hard". Shortly thereafter, Miss Olmsted surprised them with a week's pay, four days off and all arrangements made at the Carmack Motel in the French section of Montreal, Canada. The result was a bouncy, healthy baby boy they named Dewey. The Fisher's insist Dewey was Miss Olmsted's idea, and he was welcomed at the Inn any time Lois couldn't find a babysitter. (Wallington 1982, 76-82)

Meeting Betty DeMent, a former waitress at the Normandy Inn, provided a lot of insight into the experience of working at the restaurant. During her interview, Betty told me she had worked during high school and for a couple of years after she graduated, 1950-1958. Betty was hired by Katherine Olmsted and reports that she was good to work for. Very strict, you had to do things her way, but everything ran well. The busiest times were Easter and Mother's Day. Betty remembers working after school with Louis Fisher and anytime they needed her. Betty said she made twenty-five cents an hour but the tips were where you made your money. Betty saved up and bought her first car, a 1955 beige and blue Chevy Belair.

**Betty DeMent's first car purchased with tip money, 1955 Chevy Belair**
*Betty DeMent*

Betty continued to tell me about her time working at Normandy Inn. She said that people came from all over, Syracuse and Rochester. There were a lot of special meetings like Rotary Club and wedding receptions. Katherine held a Halloween party every year for the community kids with games, gifts and candy.

The building looked like old rough antiques – it was in a barn, it wasn't sleek and new like a diner. There was an entry way with wicker chairs, where guests could sit and wait to for a table. The entrance had a circular drive for guests to be dropped off and it was landscaped with flowers. People parked along the road, there wasn't a parking lot in the 50's that Betty recalls. Katherine sat at a desk in the front entry area and there was nothing that she missed. It was a great control station for the restaurant.

When we came in for work we had to polish the French copper coffee dripolators. These were individual containers, tall with copper on the top and glass on the bottom. Each coffee was individually prepared and we cleaned the dripolators regularly. There were two shifts for the waitresses, 10am-4pm and 4pm – 9pm as the Inn served both lunch and dinner.

**Individual French**
**coffee dripolater**
*Rita Kilpatrick private*
*collection*

Betty reports the uniforms were white peasant blouses and a black pinafore. As Betty and I perused pictures of her and her twin, Carol, we noticed that the waitress uniforms changed a bit from the 1940's to the 1950's. There were no longer hats and the pinafore had less straps in the bib area. (DeMent 2023)

Twins Betty Lou and Carol Ann Vanderzille wearing Normandy Inn
waitress uniforms circa 1954
*Betty Vanderzille DeMent*

# 13

Unofficial Normandy Inn
Recipes

These recipes are unofficial and unauthorized. They are not authorized, approved, licensed or endorsed by Katherine Olmsted or Normandy Inn. The recipes presented in this chapter have similar ingredients and were selected from French recipes found in vintage cookbooks from the 1930s era. Some recipes were provided by interviewees, scrapbook or local newspaper.

In May 2013, my husband, Rich, and I went to dinner at the Normandy Inn. A scrap book of the Inn going back to the origins was on display, by Rita Kilpatrick, for public viewing. Inside the scrapbook was a typed recipe for French Onion Soup. Permission was given freely to copy the recipe. The scrapbook was made available to local patrons for over fifty odd years and the French Onion Soup recipe has since become common knowledge in the area.

<u>Soup a l'Oignon</u>
6 medium sized red onions
2 TBL margarine
8 cups cold chicken stock (2 quarts)

8 pieces of white bread, crusts removed
Margarine
½ cup grated Parmesan cheese

Peel onions and slice thinly. Sauté in margarine over low heat, for about 10 minutes, or until golden brown. Stir several times to cook evenly. Add cold soup stock, bring to a boil, reduce heat and simmer covered for 20 minutes. Serve soup in oven safe bowls. Place a slice of toasted bread on top of each bowl, topped with margarine and cheese and place under broiler until cheese is bubbly. Serves 8 (Normandy Inn Scrap Book, 2013)

So you may ask why margarine is listed in the recipe and not butter? Butter was rationed during World War II which led to a shortage of butter. State side homes were using oleomargarine or oleo for short. This was shared with me by my grandmother, Marguerite Wilson, who was a young housewife during World War II.

My great grandmother, Maude Brill, used to say, "The soup on the hob for when you are ready." What is a hob? "The hob is a flat metal shelf at the side or back of a fireplace, having its surface level with the top of the grate and used especially for heating pans" (Dictionary.com unabridged. Based on the Random House Unabridged Dictionary. "hob" accessed March 13, 2023, https://www.dictionary. com/ browse/ hob). Maude Brill was born in November 1885, a little more than 2 years before "Katherine Olmsted was born, February 1888" (National Archives 1978, file 1 of 2, 153). These ladies were born around the same time period and Katherine probably would have understood what was meant by keeping the soup on the hob, for when you are ready.

**Miss Olmsted at the Soup Toreen 1945**
*Sodus Historical Society*

"Salade a la Franca is served in the French manner of placing greens, toppings and dressing family style on the table and letting diners help themselves. This course would be served with rolls after the soup" (Berholzheimer 1938, 312). A special mention is made to "the Normandy dressing from the original French recipe" by Hamilton B. Allen in his news article. (Allen 1968) Many restaurants still today develop their own House Dressing. The following recipe for Normandy House Dressing was shared by Donna D'Ercole Douglas. She said that "Dorothy Norris made this recipe by the gallons during the height of their operation" (D'Ercole 2023).

<u>Normandy House Dressing or French Dressing</u>
½ - 1 can tomato soup
1/3 cup sugar or honey
¾ cup apple cider vinegar
1 tsp. paprika
1 tsp. grated onion or onion flakes

1 tsp celery seed
½ tsp. garlic flakes
1 tsp salt
1-2 Tablespoons Worcestershire sauce

Mix thoroughly and refrigerate. Adjust to taste for sweetness. The salad dressing should have a thin consistency. (D'Ercole 2023)

Based on this recorded comment, "Ethel's homemade rolls were the best ever tasted in these parts (Wallington 1982, 78)", below is an excellent recipe for homemade yeast rolls.

<u>Parker House Rolls</u>
2 cups milk
5 TBL Crisco
3 TBL sugar
2 tsp salt
2 yeast cakes, or packages
4 TBL lukewarm water (not hot)
6-7 cups sifted flour

Heat milk and add Crisco, sugar and salt. When lukewarm add the yeast cakes dissolved in lukewarm water. Add 2 cups of flour and beat thoroughly. Cover and set in a warm place to rise until light – about 1 ½ hours. Add enough flour to make a firm dough. Knead on a lightly floured board until smooth and elastic to touch. Cover and set in a warm place to rise until double in bulk. Knead again. Roll the dough to one inch thickness and cut with a large round cutter. Brush each piece with softened Crisco. Mark through the center with the back of a knife and fold over. Place rolls on a greased shallow pan 1 inch apart. Cover and set in a warm place to rise until double in size. Bake in a hot oven 400 degrees for 15-20 minutes. Makes 2 ½ dozen rolls (Splint 1920, 134)

Menus were commonly taken as souvenirs. Dom D'ercole was quoted as saying, "...If you must take home a souvenir menu, ask for the smaller version (Allen 1968)." Donna D'Ercole Douglas shared a copy of the Normandy Inn menu from 1960 with me. Based on the menu," Le Couquille St. Jacques is a standard appetizer included with the meal." (Normandy Inn Menu 1960) The French translation for couquille is shell. The Saint Jacques Couquille is a large scallop that is found in the ocean. If you search Coquilles Saint Jacques on the internet, many renditions of this recipe will come up. Here is a similar recipe from a 1938 cookbook.

<u>Scallops a la Françoise</u>

1 cup cooked scallops or white fish
1 cup fresh mushrooms, sliced
1 small onion, diced
1 TBL fresh parsley, chopped
3 TBL margarine
1 cup milk
Salt & pepper to taste
¼ cups buttered cracker crumbs
½ cup grated cheese
6 scallop or clam shells, scrubbed clean

In a large frying pan, sauté mushrooms, onion and parsley in margarine, about 6-10 minutes, until mushrooms are tender.

Make a white sauce or roux, a blend of flour and fat used to thicken base sauces. Blend flour into the margarine, mushrooms, onion and parsley until combined. Slowly add milk, cook until thickened stirring constantly to make a roux.

Add cut up scallops, salt and pepper to mixture, cook until fish is heated. Place in greased dishes (the Normandy Inn used clean scallop or clam shells according to many people interviewed; Jan and Pete Mastracy 2023, Donna D'Ercole Douglas 2023 Rita Kilpatrick 2023 and Amy Tindall 2023), top with buttered cracker crumbs and Parmesan cheese and brown in a hot oven 400 degrees. Serves 6 (Berolzheimer 1938, 215)

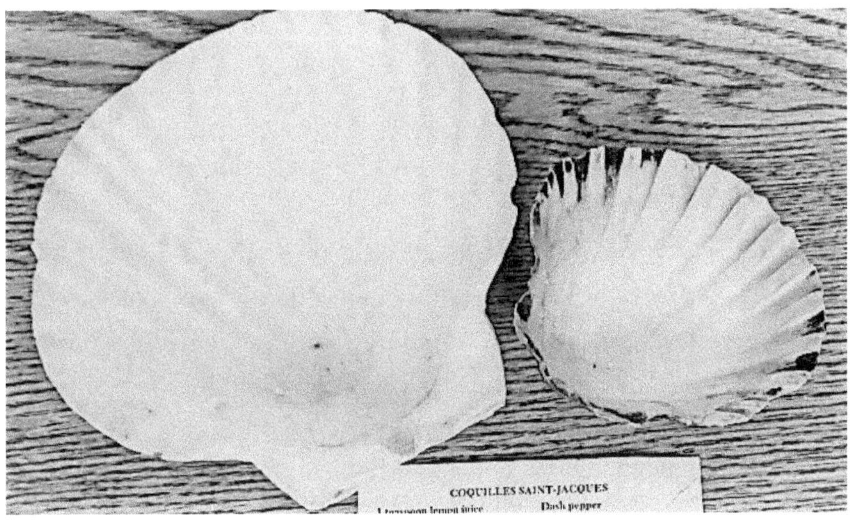


**Scallop Shells used at the Normandy Inn**
*Amy Tindall, private collection*

Vegetables would have been served with the entrée chosen. Two different vegetable dishes were offered and great care was taken in their preparation. According to Dom D'Ercole, "so many order the second vegetable just because it's on the menu, and send it back to the kitchen untouched that we are considering serving a one-vegetable meal. It's a shame to waste good food after we've fussed with it to make it the very best" (Allen 1968).

Consulting the 1938 cookbook section on French recipes, it states, "The Institute secured these excellent recipes directly from French kitchens. One of the secrets of French cooking is the use of a whiff of garlic. Even if it does not appear in the recipe, the bowl, baking dish or food is usually rubbed with it" (Berolzheimer 1938, 615). Perhaps this secret was used in the vegetable dishes?

Hollandaise sauce will give asparagus or other vegetables a French accent. Here is that recipe from the same cookbook and is delicious over vegetables.

<u>Hollandaise Sauce</u>
2 egg yolks
½ cup butter or margarine
¼ tsp salt
Dash cayenne
1 TBL lemon juice

Place egg yokes with 1/3 butter in top of double boiler. Keep water in bottom of boiler hot but not boiling. Stir eggs and butter constantly, continue adding portions of butter, stirring and waiting until melted before adding more. When mixture is thick, remove from heat and add other ingredients. (Berolzheimer 1938, 312)

According to a vintage Normandy Inn menu, the special dessert menu during Katherine's ownership had "Orange Supreme listed, a kind of orange hollowed out with orange sherbet and other stuff inside, topped with an amazing meringue. It was hot and cold at the same time" (Normandy Inn Menu 1943). Here is a recipe for Orange Baked Alaska, which is quite similar.

<u>Orange Baked Alaska</u>
1 pint orange sherbet
6 oranges
Save the orange pieces and dice them up
½ cup sliced almonds
½ cup maraschino cherries, cut into quarters
3 egg whites

6 TBL granular sugar
¼ tsp cream of tartar


Scoop the orange sherbet into 6 balls and place them on a plate. Freeze until very firm, at least 4 hours. Wash oranges and cut around the edge with a small knife. Remove the fruit and membrane, reserving the fruit for filling. Save the orange shells for filling.

Place the orange shells on a baking sheet. Mix together the diced orange pieces, almonds and maraschino cherries and place mixture in the bottom of each orange shell.

Preheat oven to 450 degrees. In a clean glass or metal bowl, whip egg whites with an electric mixer until foamy. Mix in cream of tartar and gradually beat in the sugar while continuing to whip until stiff and glossy.

Place a ball of sherbet into each orange shell, on top of diced orange mixture. Cover the sherbet with meringue, sealing the edges of the orange peel.

Bake for 5 minutes in preheated over, until browned. Remove and serve immediately. (KARLA10, 2020)


And another great dessert recipe was published in the Record newspaper in 1984. It sounds like the elegant little cookies which were served in the 1950s. Just the sort of flourish that must have made dining at the Normandy Inn a unique experience.

According to Dorothy Norris, Head Cook, in a 1984 news article, "The Normandy Inn was serving these little cookies with a dish of ice cream when I began working there some 34 years ago. They were real popular and what's nice about them is that they will last a long time. Years ago, when we served large quantities, we made large batches and stored them in 30 gallon tins." (Norris 1984, 3)

<u>Ice Cream Cookie</u>
1 cup butter (real butter, no substitutes)
½ cup powdered sugar
1 egg yolk
2 ½ cups flour
2 tsp. vanilla

Soften the butter. It must be real soft because this is a very thick mixture. Add the powdered sugar to softened butter and mix. Then add the egg yolk, flour and vanilla, in that order, mixing after adding each ingredient.

Squeeze this mixture through a pastry bag onto a cookie sheet. At the Normandy, we used to fill the center with about a fourth of a Maraschino cherry. You can do this or use some other decoration for the center or just leave it plain. Bake ten minutes at 350 degrees.

If you don't have a pastry bag, you can just drop them onto a cookie sheet by the teaspoonful. But they are prettier by using a pastry bag as they are fluted. (Norris 1984, 3)

The dough would be pressed through a pastry bag, drawn in a circle shape like a wreath. Similar results can be achieved with a cookie press.

# 14

Unfortunate End Of An Era

Rita Kilpatrick shared a business summary of the Normandy Inn, Sodus, NY, which was prepared by Katherine Olmsted in September 1963. It appeared as if Katherine were preparing to list the business for sale. The business summary states, in part,

> The Normandy Inn had its' 36th season in 1963 and was opened in 1927. Each year the Inn increased its patronage and prestige and has been operating at full capacity. There is very complete equipment to serve 300 people per day. Up to 500 dinners were served on high event days, such as Mother's Day. The Inn has a large reception room, two dining rooms; the larger seating 200 and the smaller seating 40. Adjoining there is also a very nice cottage for the owner or manager, with three bedrooms, two living rooms, bathroom and kitchenette.
>
> There is a parking lot for over 300 cars. The place is nicely landscaped and most charming inside and out. The large second floor has been given over to a gift shop and Rural Women's Exchange. (K. Olmsted Business Summary 1963)

The Business Summary sounded like an advertisement and we wondered if Katherine had been thinking of selling the Normandy Inn after 36 successful years.  Katherine was 75 years old at the time she wrote the Business Summary.

As things worked out, Katherine did not have to witness the sale of her beloved restaurant. Sadly she passed away in April 1964, soon after her 76 birthday, and just as the Inn reopened in the spring.  Thankfully, her illness was brief according to the newspaper announcement below. Her death certificate "lists her age 76 years and Cardiac Arrhythmia as cause of death," on file at the Town Clerk Office in Sodus, N.Y. (Sodus Town Clerk 1964) Katherine's obituary contains more information, and was printed in the local paper, The Record.

## DEATH CLAIMS FOUNDER OF NORMANDY INN

Miss Katherine Olmsted of Sodus died at Myers Community Hospital April 7, 1964 after a brief illness.  1963 was the 36th season of her popular Normandy Inn of Sodus.

She is survived by her sister-in-law, Mrs. Harry L. Olmsted of Sodus and two cousins, Mrs. William C. Parks of Alton and Miss Anna W. Olmsted of Syracuse.

Funeral services were held Friday afternoon with Rev. Richard Cahoon officiating.  Burial will be in Brick Church Cemetery, Sodus Center, at the convenience of the family.

Contributions may be made in her memory to Myers Community Hospital building fund. (Death Claims Founder 1964, 1)

Katherine Olmsted's Last Will and Testament is filed at the Wayne County Clerk's office and states "the entire estate and belongings are inherited by her cousin, Miss Anna Wetherill Olmsted." (Wayne County Clerk 1964, 520)

This book summarizes some of Katherine Olmsted's major accomplishments.  She was a dedicated nurse for 14 years, survived World War I and received many medals in honor for her service.  She dreamed big and developed a new life course as a Cordon Bleu Chef and later Owner of the Normandy Inn. Katherine continued to give talks and write articles on nursing, safety, cooking and the origins of the Normandy Inn. In the process of pursuing her life's dream, she impacted an entire community with her kindness and provided employment to many families over a 36 year time span. This was not an easy task during the Great Depression when unemployment was high and people could not find jobs. Her vision for the Normandy Inn became enormously popular and had far appeal, well throughout the states and beyond. She was a person who accomplished so much in one lifetime. It is hopeful that others may find inspiration from the retelling of the story of Katherine Olmsted's life experience.

The Normandy Inn, a wildly successful enterprise with a strongly developed business concept, was "sold in 1965 to Dominick D'Ercole" (Wayne County Clerk 1965, 841).

**Katherine Olmsted 1888 - 1964**
*Sodus Historical Society*

*Normandy Inn*
*Owner, Operator*
*Dominick D'Ercole*
*1965 - 1999*

# 15

# Carrying On A Tradition

According to the Wayne County Clerk's office, "Miss Anna Wether-ill Olmsted, executor of Katherine Olmsted's estate, sold the Normandy Inn to Dominick D'Ercole of Lyons in 1965"(Wayne County Clerk 1965, 841).

Dominic D'Ercole completed a many updates to the restaurant, such as remodeling, décor, updating the menu and hours of operation. The Arms Crossroads- Wallington provides a good summary.

> Dom and his wife, Antoinette, spent until April 7, 1967 remodeling and enlarging the inn. They converted the home to the east into a bar, sealed off the trim pantry, and closed off the upper loft area. The décor and peasant costumes have remained the same along with several favorites on the menu. At a quick glance the exterior looks much as it did when Miss Olmsted owned it but the gardens and pond had been sacrificed for more parking area. The Inn has now been restored to its original grandeur. One major change the new owners made is that the Inn is now open year round. (Wallington 1982, 82)

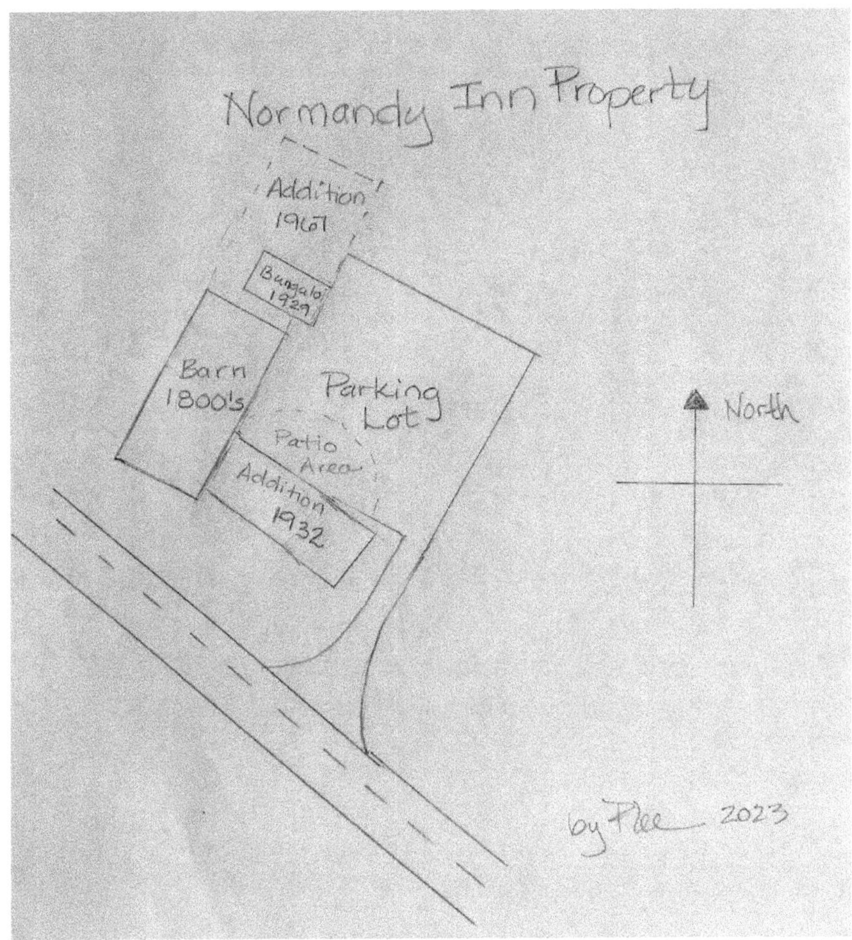


**Normandy Inn property additions over the years**
*Sketch by Pamela Lee*

The barn was originally built in the 1800s and the small bungalow in the reaar is  first mentioned in 1929, and later described by Katherine as a very nice cottage with three bedrooms, two living rooms, bathroom and kitchenette.  The community came together in 1932 and built the new dining wing, that faces the main road.  D'Ercole enclosed the cottage in an addition and added the parking lot in 1967.

**Normandy Inn front entrance, 1970s**
*Donna D'Ercole Douglas*

Pete Mastracy, a friend of Dom D'Ercole and regular diner, provided information about the renovations.

> Dom did a tremendous job renovating the Normandy Inn after he bought it. He added on the new banquet room and a walk in cooler. Neil Fitzgerald did the refrigeration work at the Inn. The bar was located in the wing of the restaurant, along the front of the building. The second floor of the main dining room had storage and was open in the center with a railing, looking into the downstairs. "Standing on the first floor in the restaurant, you could look up to the roof of the original building." (Mastracy 2023)

A newspaper article by Hamilton B. Allen, a Syracuse Food Critic, provides further details about the extensive remodeling.

> Dom connected the farm house with the inn and used the space for a cocktail lounge and bar. The entrance was moved and a stone patio recently constructed, among other changes. Dom has, however, allowed the dining rooms to remain as Miss Olmsted created them except for the new carpeted concrete floor which replaces the creaky old wooden floor of the main room. The beamed ceilings, the small paned French windows, the huge fireplace with its great copper pots and pans and collection of priceless antiques add old-world appeal. (Allen 1968)

Edson Ennis, Wayne County History Museum Board Member, located Donna D'Ercole Douglas, who is Dominic D'Ercole's daughter, and encouraged her contribution to this book. In an interview with Donna, she shared quite a bit about her Dad, the Normandy Inn and also her time serving as a waitress upon occasion.

> Donna told me a cute story of how Dorothy Norris and Dom D'Ercole met on a hot, sweaty day. Dom was at the property, working on structural improvements to the building just after he purchased the Normandy Inn. Up drove Dorothy and her husband Bud in an old red farm pick-up truck. Dom thought, what is this? Looks like some farmhands looking for work. A sweet little lady hopped out and said, woohoo, woohoo! It was Dorothy Norris who had begun work as a young girl for Miss Olmsted, cleaning and working in the Country Store. Over the years Dorothy was promoted to pastry assistant and food prep in the kitchen. She had the recipes of the Normandy Inn in her head and heart. Well, Dom couldn't pass up this opportunity and he hired her on the spot as the head cook.
> Dorothy prepared some beautiful breads, roast young duckling and the famous Normandy House salad dressing.

Turns out, Dom and Dorothy were quite a team and created some delicious meals over the years. While in the kitchen working and getting the food cooked, Dom called Dorothy "Norris", but when introducing her in the restaurant he called her by her first name.

Donna told me that under Dom's guidance, the Normandy Inn was a true family enterprise during his ownership. Donna's Mom, Toni as she was known to friends, was hostess and waitress. Donna herself worked as waitress, hostess and even bartender when needed. Her brother Gregory D'Ercole ran the dishwasher and cleaned. Donna's cousin, Michael Alvaro, worked as bartenders and her cousin, Tammy Alvaro, worked as a bus girl and server if needed.

Donna identified the peasant dress from the 1950s as the one she also wore when waitressing for her Dad in the 1970s, which was the waitress uniform designed by Katherine Olmsted. Donna said her Dad was committed to carrying on the tradition of the Normandy Inn. Two murals in the dining room were there when Dad bought the place. We cleaned them and touched up the paint in spots, but did not make any other changes. (D'Ercole 2023)

Some regular staff, unfortunately, did not return to the Normandy Inn when it reopened. The Record notes that "Miss Alice Bourne, harpist, did not return after Miss Olmsted's passing" (Recordings 1965, 4).

Allen, mentioned in his article that "Mrs. Norris carried on the tradition of fine cooking and had been taught by Miss Olmsted. Mrs. Norris had been at the inn 26 years" (Allen 1968). His article described D'eErcole's menu in the late 1960s in the selection below.

Items remaining on the menu include roast duck, veal cutlet, French onion soup, Le Coquille St. Jacques; served hot from the broiler with every meal just after the salad; the Normandy dressing from the original French recipe, fresh cukes in sour cream and the green beans with ham bits all recalled frequent, pleasurable visits to the inn in the 1930s and '40s.

Allen quoted Dom as saying, "so many order the second vegetable, just because it's on the menu, and send it back to the kitchen untouched that I'm considering serving a one-vegetable meal. It's a shame to waste good food after we've fussed with it to make it the very best." And he has a rule, no Italian dishes served on the premises. "I went all the way and took them off the menu in order to continue the inn as Miss Olmsted intended". (Allen 1968)

Allen goes on to say that "Dom carried on another Olmsted tradition, serving High School French Class students lunch. Mrs. Norris would cook a French-style menu with chicken a la Normandy featured" (Allen 1968). French inspired dinners were a great opportunity for local French class students to have an "eatertainment" experience without traveling to France. Apparently, they would serve the French Class students in groups, by classrooms on different days.  However, the hours of business were different under D'Ercole's ownership.

According to Allen in 1968, the Inn was closed on Tuesdays, and served luncheons and dinners the other days of the week. As of this date, seating was available without reservations.

Allen's article quoted Dom in his humorous way of speaking, "To make it a pleasant two-way deal, pleasant for guest and for the host, eat your plate clean, don't steal the shells on which le coquille St. Jacques is served and if you must take home a souvenir menu, ask for the smaller version. (Allen 1968)

Banquets,
Parties,
Luncheons

# Appetizers

Tomato Juice  .50  Fruit Cup .75
French Onion Soup & Soup du Jour  1.00
Jumbo Shrimp Cocktail  $3.50
Antipasto  $2.75

# Half Portion Dinners
## for children up to 7 years

Chopped Sirloin
Turkey
Ham
Your Choice $2.50

# Desserts

Tarts  .65        Ice Cream  .60
Parfaits .85      Sherbert - .60
       Homemade  Pies  - .95

# Beverages

Coffee  .40       Milk  .30
Sanka  .40          large .60
Tea  .40          Cola .50

# Special
Open Steak Sandwich - French Fries $6.95

# Entrees

## From the broiler —

Prime Ribs of Beef - au jus          9.50
Ladies Cut Prime Rib   -   7.50
New York Cut Sirloin   -   8.95
Thick Pork Chops       -   7.50
Virginia Ham Steak     -   6.50
Surf and Turf          -   18.95

## Roast perfection —

Long Island Duckling       7.50
Turkey with Dressing       6.95
Cornish Hen            -    6.50
Coq au Vin - chicken in wine s    5.50
Veal Cutlet - tomato Sauce    7.50

## From the seas —

Alaskan King Crab - lemon, butt    18.95
Lobster Tails - drawn butter       18.95
Deep Fried Shrimp - tartar sau     7.95
Fillet of Haddock - (Fridays       4.50
Seafood Platter - shrimp, scallops, h    8.95
Coquille St. Jacques               5.95
Breaded Scallops                   7.95

Entrees include relish tray,
Coquille St. Jacques, potato,
rolls and butter - Blue chee

Pete and Jan Mastracy dined regularly at the Normandy Inn under Dominic D'Ercole's ownership and they recalled their time spent there.

> During Pete Mastracy's interview, he said that he and his wife Jan dined regularly at the Normandy Inn in the late 1970s when Dom D'Ercole and his wife Toni owned the restaurant. Dom continued to serve the Coquille St. Jacques appetizer, introduced by the prior owner Katherine Olmsted. The appetizer was served on a good sized ocean shell, about 4"-5" across. Dom was an excellent cook, previously he owned the Dolphin restaurant in Sodus Point. Dom made an excellent prime rib and his wife Toni waited tables at the Normandy.
>
> Pete said that Dom was an interesting character. He had a collection of equipment and items behind the Normandy Inn. Not to call this a junk pile, he seriously had plans for all the equipment and turned down any offers if someone wanted to buy something. He was an excellent cook but really disliked the paperwork of owning a business. Dom once told the story of being audited by the IRS. The agent asked to see his books, so he went into the kitchen and filled up a box of dinning receipts. Dom brought the box out and dumped the receipt pile on the table. The agent said, "What am I supposed to do with this?" and he replied, "There is nothing in the law that says I have to be neat". (Mastracy 2023)

A newspaper article printed in the Record on September 25, 1975 states that "the Normandy Inn is a joint venture of Dominic D'Ercole and Dorothy Norris, whom he refers to as his culinary expert." (The Normandy Inn 1975, 2)

Dominic D'Ercole and Dorothy Norris, September 25, 1975
*The Record, Sodus, New York*

The news article highlights Dorothy Norris' and Dom D'Ercole's working partnership.

The dedicated pair have continued the old tradition of the inn. The changes have been largely structural, but nothing to detract from the old world charm. The accent is still French, although not strictly so. Dom frowns on Italian items and you won't find any on the menu. Dom is quoted as saying, "There are a great many Italian type restaurants and we prefer to restrict our menus to French and American dishes."

The article goes on to state that D'Ercole carried on the tradition of the complimentary Coquille St. Jacques and specially selected wines. He is quoted as saying, "One dines at the Normandy Inn. We are not going to be steam table operation ever." (The Normandy Inn 1975, 2)

Donna D'Ercole Douglas described her Dad during her interview.

Donna summed up her Dad's attributes as dedicated, charming, open, welcoming, and very old fashioned. He would kiss the ladies hands and call everyone "Alice" jokingly as he couldn't remember their names. He was polite and funny. Her Dad was the quintessential barman, loved socializing and chatting with customers. If he wasn't at the bar, he was preparing the entrees alongside Dorothy Norris, who made the soups and vegetables, in the kitchen. Dom was an excellent Chef and good at preparing the meats. He really cared about the restaurant and how the food was served. Dom was a perfectionist; how the table was set, how food came out of the kitchen and no spilled drinks. His trademark was the relish tray, which included celery, carrots, peppers and olives – sometimes pickles or tomatoes if in season. That relish tray went out immediately after the drink order. Then salad and rolls, handmade by Dorothy. The next course was the Normandy Inn's signature dish, Couquille St. Jacques, followed by the main course. And of course desserts followed, cream de menthe sundaes, Mrs. Norris' famous pies and peach cobbler.

Donna said her Dad was very social and welcoming to the guests and thanked people for coming. He asked how the guests liked everything, food, service, etc. And he appreciated all of the workers. (D'Ercole 2023)

**Dom and Toni D'Ercole dancing**
*Donna D'Ercole Douglas*

Things had been going well for just over twelve years and then the Normandy Inn suffered a fire. The Record states that

> "the January 6, 1980 fire was caused by electrical wiring near the kitchen area. The Wayne County Sheriff's Department Investigator stated that the heat and smoke caused extensive damage to the inside of the building. Sadly, one of the German Shepherd watchdogs perished in the fire, but there were no other injuries. (Historic Normandy Inn Burns 1980, 1&5)

Normandy Inn fire damage 1980
*Donna D'Ercole Douglas*

Pete Mastracy discussed the fire, the cause, and what the fellows worked on during the property cleanup.

Pete said that the fire in 1980 was determined to have been caused by electrical issues. Being friends with Dom, he offered to help him clean up afterward. He said the fire damaged primarily the bar area and a part of the restaurant. The laminate top of the bar burnt off and they had to put a new top on. The beautiful old beams used in the structure were very thick, but singed badly on the exterior. It was determined that the original beams could remain in place and be salvaged by sand blasting, essentially taking a layer off the top. In typical Dom fashion, he arranged to borrow two questionable looking sand blasters, one running on a generator and the other on gas, as the electricity to the building was turned off. The work was hot and challenging as they had to wear suits and be totally masked up. Pete said they couldn't see due to the dust, so they sent in two workers at a time, with one holding a light and the other sandblasting. The men worked in half-hour shifts, sending the other work pair in after thirty minutes. Once the sandblasting was done, the wooden beams looked beautiful and showed the wood grain. Dom had a guy come in and apply new stain on the beams with an air sprayer. The Inn looked good after the clean-up but it took quite a bit of time to get rid of the smoke smell. (Mastracy 2023)

The Record reported that "the Normandy Inn re-opened about two months after the fire, when clean up completed. The paper also said that great progress was made on the remodeling" (Jim Colucci 1980, 5).

But then, another go around with fire occurred at the Normandy Inn "for the second time within two years. This time Dom noticed the fire and pulled the fire alarm" (Jim Colucci 1982, 1).

The local paper, The Record, reports that Wallington, Sodus, Sodus Point, Sodus Center, Alton and Lyons fire departments responded with 125 firemen and fought the blaze for nearly four hours. Wallington Fire Chief Ken Eastley said, When we arrived (just moments after the call) flames were rolling out of the windows. We had it pretty much under control in an hour and a half. No one was injured, but by the time the fire was out, the inside of the Inn was destroyed. Mrs. D'Ercole said she didn't know if her husband planned to rebuild or not. Chief Eastley said the Wallington Volunteer Fire Department and the Wayne County Sheriffs Arson Task Force would be investigating the cause of the fire, although he said he has no reason to suspect arson. (Jim Colucci 1982, 1)

After 6 months the clean- up and repair was completed the second time and the Normand Inn was back in business. "The Record begins reporting dinners and meetings held at the Normandy in in early February 1983" (Jim Colucci 1983, 11)

Donna D'Ercole Douglas told me about the last few years that her Dad owned the Normandy Inn.

When Route 104 was relocated in the 1980's, parallel and east of the Normandy Inn, the traffic reduced and resulted in a decline in restaurant customers. As the years wore on, customer traffic continued to drop-off. It was after this, around 1992, that Dorothy Norris retired and they stopped serving dinners. Dom just loved the property and was still out there every day. He kept the bar open for regulars and made lunches for the Dynalec workers in Sodus for a time.

In 1997, Dad unexpectedly passed away. The Normandy Inn property sat vacant from 1997 to 1999 waiting for the next owners. (D'Ercole 2023)

*Normandy Inn*
*Owner, Operator*
*Rita Kilpatrick and*
*Michael Wasson*
*1999 - 2020*

# 16

# Keeper of the History

## KEEPER OF THE HISTORY

According to the Wayne County Clerk's Office, "on February 16, 1999 Rita Kilpatrick and Michael Wasson purchased 7639 Ridge Road, Sodus from the Estate of Dominick D'Ercole (Wayne County Clerk 1999, 748)".

The following pictures of the Normandy Inn were provided by Rita Kilpatrick. They display what the property looked like in 1999 when Kilpatrick and Wasson were ready to open for business. There are two pictures of the exterior and two pictures of the interior.

Normandy Inn front entrance 1999
*Rita Kilpatrick*

Normandy Inn building facing the road 1999
*Rita Kilpatrick*

**Normandy Inn main dining room 1999**
*Rita Kilpatrick*

**Normandy Inn bar 1999**
*Rita Kilpatrick*

During an interview with Rita Kilpatrick, the third owner of the Normandy Inn, and her daughter, Amy Tindall, they shared some of the history during their ownership of the property.

Rita told me that Dominic D'Ercole had been talking to her and Mike Wasson about purchasing the Inn from him for some time. Rita had worked at Tom Jones in Lyons for ten years and had experience with bar and food service. Rita confirmed that they purchased the business in February 1999 and re-opened the Normandy Inn to the public on April 29, 1999. There was quite a lot of clean-up to the building and grounds that was done. Dom had amassed a lot of equipment over the years, even built some lien-tos to house the items. They had an auction to sell off the pieces outside, including a material press machine and fifteen cars. The space was then opened up for parking. Business volume started out slowly in the beginning, but really took off once the liquor license was in place. Dorothy Norris, former cook under the tutelage of Miss Olmsted and later cook for Dominic D'Ercole, made a special visit to show Rita and Mike how to make the signature appetizer, Coquille St. Jacques. Amy confirmed that they served Coquille St. Jacques on an oyster shell complimentary with diners. The number of diners slowed down when New York State implemented the indoor smoking bans.

Rita and Mike employed quite a few family members over the years. Rita's sister, Joyce Vitaro, was hostess and her other sister, Gloria Garafano, was waitress. Rita's daughters worked at the Inn as well, Terri Meeks as waitress and Amy Tindall doing whatever was needed; waitress, cook or bartender. Granddaughter Miranda Almekinder helped bartend and grandson Adriaan Sergeant was dishwasher. Rita trained Miranda how to make change when collecting payments, a very useful life skill. Mike Wasson was Head Cook and Cristina Vitaro was also a cook.

A longtime friend, Barb Gay, also served as waitress. This team hosted many wedding, banquets and receptions over the years.

Both Rita and Amy shared stories about the fun times they had hosting various Halloween and Pajama parties at Normandy Inn. (Kilpatrick & Tindall 2023)

An article written by Christina Russell, a food critic for The Sun and Record, provided a summary of the re-opened Normandy Inn.

The Normandy Inn is owned by Rita Kilpatrick and hours of operation are Tuesday – Sunday. Soft music is played over speakers and Rita also serves as bartender. Rita maintains the old scrap book from when Miss Olmsted owned the inn and a guest book from 1958. The regular menu included many items of chicken, beef, pork, seafood and Italian choices, even pizza. A complimentary appetizer is served with every meal, called co-quille. The coquille was rich and cheesy with seafood in it. She also brought very soft delicious rolls and salad covered in pepper Parmesan dressing. The Normandy Inn is available to book wedding parties and special social events. (Russell 2009, 6)

Miranda Almekinder, Rita's granddaughter, provided information about the mural that was painted when Rita and Michael owned the Normandy Inn.

The mural in the bar area, located in the middle of the two pre-existing murals, was painted by Melissa Plouse and includes the following people within the scene; Amy Tindall, waitress, Carl Fowler, seated at the bar, Adriaan Sargent, little boy, Rita Kilpatrick, on phone behind the bar, Tim Almekinder, seated, Michael Wasson, behind the bar and Miranda Almekinder, little girl. There is a calendar in the mural with the date April 29, 1999 highlighted, which is the date they reopened the restaurant and bar. (Miranda Almekinder 2023)

**Mural added during the 3rd ownership of the restaurant 1999**
*Photo by Pamela Lee, courtesy of Terri Sanford & Erin Atkins, building owners*
*2023*

# Normandy Inn

108  -  PAMELA LEE

Banquets          Parties          Luncheons

## Appetizers

| | | |
|---|---|---|
| Shrimp Cocktail | $6.95 | Cheese Stix  $4 |
| Clams Casino | $5.95 | French Onion  Bowl  $2 |
| Coquille Platter | $5.95 | Cup  $2 |
| Stuffed Mushrooms (Crab Stuffing) | $5.95 | |
| Chicken Fingers | $4.95 | |

Soup DeJour   Cup   $1.50
Bowl   $1.95

## Salads

| | |
|---|---|
| Grilled Chicken or Steak in a Bread Bowl | $5.95 |
| Caesar Grilled Chicken or anchovies | $5.95 |
| Julienne Ham, Turkey & Cheese | $5.95 |
| Tossed Garden Salad | $1.95 |

## Beverages

| | | | |
|---|---|---|---|
| Coffee | $0.75 | Milk | $1.00 |
| Tea | $0.75 | Soft Drink | $1.00 |

**Fully Stocked Bar**

## Entrees

### Prime Rib of Beef - Au Jus

**Petite Cut** $10.95     **Reg. cut** $15.95     **Normandy Cut** $19.9

| | |
|---|---|
| New York Strip Steak (14 - 16 oz.) | $15.95 |
| Porter House Steak ( 20 oz.) | $19.95 |
| Grilled Pork Chops | $9.95 |
| Breaded Pork Chops | $9.95 |
| Grilled Ham Steak | $9.95 |

## Poultry

| | |
|---|---|
| Country Fried Chicken | $8.95 |
| Broiled Half Chicken | $8.95 |
| Grilled Marinated Chicken Breast | $9.95 |
| Grilled or Lemon Pepper Chicken Breast | $9.95 |
| Grilled Cajun Chicken Breast | $9.95 |

# Normandy Inn

MISS OLMSTED'S NORMANDY INN  -  109

**Banquets**          **Parties**          **Luncheons**

## Seafood

| | |
|---|---|
| Haddock Fillet Deep Fried or Broiled | $8.95 |
| Sea Scallops Deep Fried or Broiled | $13.95 |
| Shrimp Deep Fried or Broiled | $13.95 |
| Seafood Platter Deep Fried or Broiled | |
| ( Fish, Scallops, & Shrimp) | $15.95 |
| Stuffed Haddock | |
| (stuffed with crab meat dressing) | $13.95 |
| | |
| Alaskan King Crab with drawn butter | $21.95 |
| Lobster Tail Single    ~ 8oz | $21.95 |
| Lobster Tail Double    ~ 8 oz ea. | $34.95 |
| "Captains Platter": | $19.95 |

(Stuffed Haddock, Stuffed shrimp, & Clams Casino)

## Italian Dishes

| | |
|---|---|
| Spaghetti or Ziti w/ meatballs | $6.95 |
| Spaghetti or Ziti w/ mushrooms | $7.50 |
| Spaghetti or Ziti w/sausage | $7.50 |
| Spaghetti w/oil & garlic | $6.95 |
| Veal Parmesan | $11.95 |
| Chicken Parmesan | $10.95 |
| Cheese Ravioli w/meatballs | $9.50 |
| Cheese Ravioli w/sausage | $9.95 |

All Entrees include:
Salad, Coquille St. Jacques,
Potato or Pasta, Bread and butter.

*Separate checks not available for Parties of 8 or more.

My husband, Rich and I dinned at the Normandy Inn in May 2013. The scrap book was shared with us, containing all the wonderful history of the Inn, news clippings, recipes and visits from famous persons of yore. It was clear that the current owners sought to maintain the history of the place. Two peasant waitress uniforms hung on the doors in the main dining room and a complimentary Coquille Saint Jacques was offered with our dinner. The menu contained American dishes and the food was very good. The patio entrance area had been kept up with cheerful flowers and gnomes playfully scattered, which was quite pleasant. "Rita told me that she and her sister had painted the gnomes.

**Normandy Inn back entrance to banquet hall 2013**
*Photographed by Pamela Lee*

Rita said she and Mike retired in 2017 and what she misses the most are the customers and people that visited. The property sat vacant for a few years, waiting for the next owner" (Kilpatrick & Tindall, 2023).

*Normandy Inn*
*Auction House*
*James Hoyt, Auctioneer*
*2020 — 2022*

# 17

# A Brief Interlude

According to the Wayne County Clerk's Office, "on October 16, 2020 James Hoyt purchased 7639 Ridge Road from Rita Kilpatrick and Michael Wasson" (Wayne County Clerk 2020).

Jim Hoyt shared the following information about the property during an interview.

According to Jim Hoyt, the building had sat vacant for a couple of years prior to his purchase. He assumed that they shut the restaurant down prior to selling. There was wildlife living in the building when Jim took it over, raccoons and squirrels. Intending to make this property his new auction house, he set to work. A lot of restoration work was needed in the building; new insulation, steel siding, plumbing, heating and electric upgrades. Outbuildings were taken down, which included a walk-in freezer and a walk-in cooler. There is a storage shed that he moved out back, which was originally up close to the building front when he purchased it. He also cleared away encroaching woodland brush and trees.

Jim reported that there was a water leak in one area of the roof and one wall was rotted out due to the leak and had to be replaced. The replaced wall is the one the front entrance is now located on, to the left of the door and across the room from the murals. All new, dry and safe now. The main roof only required minor repair and one chimney had to be taken down. There are four fireplaces total in the building. The fireplace in the newer back addition is no longer useable, it is aesthetic only, due to the chimney removal. The kitchen was taken out, which was located in the back of the new addition. Jim tore out all of the kitchen equipment and replaced the flooring.

Jim laughingly told me that his wife was ready to throw in the towel on this project and wondered why he had purchased the building in the first place. He said it probably would have been torn down if he had not performed the building stabilization. And he wasn't expecting to fix then sell the building so soon, but Terri was ready to take it on. And thank goodness Jim and Terri were on site to preserve this historical property.

Jim closed with the following comment, "back in the day this property had beautiful gardens out front. It really was a show place." (Hoyt 2023)

Terri Sanford and her daughter Erin Atkins, the current owners of the property, shared in an interview some of the clean-up work on the property.

Terri and Erin said they helped clean up alongside of Jim. The second floor, old hayloft, was sealed off as the floor had become unsafe. Jim also added concrete sidewalks that replaced the patio blocks out front.

The old barn facility housed Jim's auction business on one side and the Sodus Feeds & Needs store was in the newer half of the building, in back. Everyone pitched in to fix up the property, including tearing down old ceiling panels. With restorations complete, the updated building opened up in 2021. Business was doing so well for both enterprises that either one or the other had to move out to create more space. In January 2022, Jim sold the building to Terri Sanford and Erin Atkins. Jim relocated the auction house to the old Barbara Jean's furniture store in North Rose. (Sanford & Atkins 2023)

*Sodus Feeds and
Artisans Co-op
Terri Sanford & Erin Atkins
2022 – current*

# 18

# Vision to the Future

In an interview, Terri Sanford told about her work history and how she had become the current owner of the former Normandy Inn.

Terri said she had a full time career for 30 years, with Wayne County Nursing Home and then Finger Lakes DDSO, which serves people with developmental disabilities. Terri purchased the feed store in 2017, which was originally located on Route 14 in Alton. During the first five years, both she and Daughter Erin, who was a full time college student at the time, worked to keep the feed store running. That was two full time commitments for each of them, but true to their mettle they pulled it off very successfully. Terri retired from the health care industry in December 2021 and Erin completed college, which offers them more time to run their core business. (Sanford & Atkins 2023)

Laughingly, there is no down time at Sodus Feeds and Artisans Coop, these two ladies are still very busy.

In 2021 Terri and Erin changed their business model to include the Artisan's Co-op booth space and in 2022 finalized their purchase of the former Normandy Inn building. Their business name is now Sodus Feeds and Artisan's Co-op and they report business has been strong over their first year and a half of operation at the new location. They aim to host six events each year with additional vendors, food, wine/beer or cider tasting, raffles and giveaways. This provides the community opportunity to gather and share talents, good food, shopping and fun. And it doesn't stop there. Terri and Erin are very active in their community and have watched animals, trimmed pet's nails, watched children, hauled feed and more. Before the Artisan's Co-op, when there was space available in the building, they hosted Chamber meetings, Woman's Entrepreneur Group and also offered classes. (Sanford & Atkins 2023)

A stroll around the store shows farm feeds, domestic pet food, treats, toys, garden supplies, freshly frozen beef and chicken locally sourced, specialty foods, just about anything you can imagine needing for your home farm. And the Artisan's Co-op booths are a real treat. There are some vintage finds, hand crafted items of wide variety and the vendors switch up their displays with the seasons. Terri is very talented in setting up displays and changes up the store regularly to keep things fresh. These women have a thriving U-Haul business offering enclosed and open trailers and box trucks.

Terri said they have continued to improve the property with a large expansion of the driveway in every direction, removal of trees for the expanded driveway and expanded parking lot. 2023 included additional gravel fill to further grade the parking lot and driveway. They have also installed new LED lights throughout the interior, put in an overhead garage door for loading dock and moved the door in the back addition.

In 2023 they will be adding a fruit and vegetable stand. Future plans include potentially expanding the Artisan's Co-op space to the second floor, on the newer end of the building only. Erin told me that both the older barn section and the newer building in the back have second floors with open balconies in the center. When renovating, she noticed that there were hoists on the second floor ceilings above the open area to lift tables, or anything large that could not be carried up the stairs.

Terri mentioned that she would like to begin a scrap book with history of the property and a place for visitors to sign in for emailed event information. They are also tossing around the idea in the far future of becoming part of the wine trail as a stop hosting rotating wineries or breweries and music. If they do add to the building in the future, a potential meeting or classroom have been discussed. (Sanford & Atkins 2023)

Do you recall Katherine Olmsted's 1950 Good Neighbor Clinic speech about her recipe for success? "First of all," she advised, "you've got to enjoy what you're doing. Otherwise, don't bother. You have to have perseverance. Above all you need a sense of humor" (Women Support 1950, 20). With this same attitude Terri and Erin have forged ahead. At one of our first meetings, Terri told me that "you won't find any drama here. If something is wrong, we will find a way to work it out among ourselves. We are here to have fun" (Terri Sanford 2023).

This property holds good memories for the community of Sodus and Katherine Olmsted would be very proud of these two business women and their support of local area Co-op and the "Country Store" (Normandy Inn Menu 1960) concept. Thinking back to some of Katherine Olmsted's other business quotes, "Imagination Means Business" and "Can't I do it a little bit better or a little bit different" (Davis 1948, 29) it is reminiscent of Terri and Erin's efforts with their new business venture. These two women have made vast improvements and changes throughout their first years in business and it will be exciting to see what comes next!

Terri Atkins and Erin Atkins, current owners of the former
Normandy Inn building, now home of Sodus Feeds & Artisans Co-op

**2023**

*Photo by Pamela Lee*

# REFERENCES

A.F.K. 1950. "By the Way". *The Post-Standard*, (Jul 16, 1950) 17.

Allen, Hamilton B. circa 1968. "Tradition Returns to Normandy Inn". *Gannett News Service*, syndicated writer and critic, Rochester area newspaper. Article copy housed at Sodus Historical Society. (circa 1968).

Almekinder, Miranda 2023. Interview by Pamela Lee. June 5, 2023.

Bailey, Ronald H. 1978. *The Home Front: U.S.A. World War II*. Virginia: Time Life Books. (102-117)

Berolzheimer, Ruth. 1938. *The American Woman's Cookbook*. Consolidated Book Publishers, Inc. copyright 1938. 215,312 and 615.

Bugni, Bette. 2020. "Katherine Olmsted/Normandy Inn (1886-1964)". (February 13, 2020). http://townofsodushistoricalsociety.org/hamlets/wallington/katherine-olmsted/.

Colucci, Jim. 1980. "Seen and Heard from the Barber Chair". *The Record,* Sodus,(February 28, 1980) 5.

Colucci, Jim. 1982. "Normandy Inn Burns". *The Record*, Sodus, NY. Volume 86, Number 10. (June 17, 1982) 1.

Colucci, Jim. 1983. "Seen and Heard from the Barber Chair". *The Record,* Sodus, (February 15, 1983) 11.

"Country Store Excites State-Wide Interest: Guests From 30 Towns and Cities in State Are Expected At Normandy Inn Wednesday."1948. *The Record,* Sodus, NY. Volume 52 Number 13. (July 8, 1948) 1.

"Cuisine Diploma-Paris". 2023. *Le Cordon Bleu, Paris.* Accessed (May 14, 2023). https://www.cordonbleu.edu/paris/cuisine-diploma/en.

Davis, Treva. 1948. "500 Attend Women's Business Clinic Here". *Binghamton Press.* (April 30, 1948) 29.

"Death Claims Founder of the Normandy Inn". 1964. *The Record,* Sodus, NY. Volume 68, Number 1. (April 16, 1964) 1.

DeMent, Betty. 2023. Interview by Pamela Lee. April 6, 2023 and April 8, 2023.

D'Ercole Douglas, Donna. 2023. Interview by Pamela Lee. May 31, 2023 and June 6, 2023.

Elwood, Bob. 1960. "Accent on France at World Famous Normandy Inn". About Town Column, *Syracuse Post Standard.* (1960).

E.V.W. 1942. "Katherine Olmsted Announces Favored Recipes of Famous People At Museum Class". *Syracuse Herald American.* (February 22, 1942) 13.

Giuseppe, Milo. 2020. "1926: U.S. Starts Numbered Highway System". *USAToday.com.* (September 6, 2020). https://www.usatoday.com/ picture-gallery/life/ 2020/09/06/the-worlds-most-important-event-every-year-since-1920/42346845/

Googlemaps.com. Normandy, France. Accessed June 10, 2023. https://www.google.com/maps/place/Normandy,+France/@49.1203332,-1.3916838,8z/data=!3m1!4b1!4m6!3m5!1s0x47e1bd6c23f8c087:0x26f2f561148e202!8m2!3d48.8798704!4d0.1712529!16s%2Fg%2F121c9r7n?entry=ttu.

Hawks, Roy. 1963. "Charming French Atmosphere, Food at Normandy Inn". About Town Column. *Syracuse Post Standard.* (March 15, 1963) 24.

"Historic Normandy Inn Burns". 1980. *The Record*, Sodus, NY. Volume 83, Number 40. (January 10, 1980) 1 & 5.

Hoyt, James. 2023. Interview by Pamela Lee. June 6, 2023.

"Inn to be Reopened Despite Heavy Damage". 1945. *The Record*, Sodus, NY. Volume XLVIII, Number 45. (February 15, 1945) 1.

"Interesting Information from Miss Olmsted: Jassy, Roumania October 4th, 1917". *The Record*, Sodus, NY. (January 19, 1918) 6.

KARLA10. 2020. "Orange Baked Alaska". *Allrecipes.com.* (June 18, 2020) https://www.allrecipes.com/recipe/104983/orange-baked-alaska/

"Katherine Olmsted of the Red Cross." 1942. *Syracuse Museum of Fine Arts, Quarterly Bulletin* Volume 3, Number 2, Syracuse, New York. (Jan, Feb, Mar 1942) 7.

Kilpatrick, Rita and Tindall, Amy. 2023. Interview by Pamela Lee. June 19, 2023.

Lynch, Grace. 1968. "Strange War Time Journey". The Way it Used To Be column. *The Fulton Patriot.* (June 6, 1968).

"Many Residents of Oswego County Attending Fair: Several Awards Made to Women for Displays of Handiwork". 1940. *Oswego Palladium-Times.* (August 29, 1940) 2.

Marjorie. 1954. "Women in Business Receive Praise at Clinic". Shop Talk column. *Buffalo Courier-Express.* (June 9, 1954) 14.

Mastracy, Pete and Jan.2023. Interview by Pamela Lee. April 5, 2023.

"Miss Mary Lent Dies At Wallington Home". 1946. *The Record,* Sodus, NY. Volume L, Number 32. (November 14, 1946) 1.

"Miss Olmsted Dies; Owned Normandy Inn". 1964. *The Post Standard,* Syracuse, NY. (April 9, 1964) 7.

"Miss Olmsted Returns Home: Red Cross Nurse Makes Perilous Trip From Roumania to England: Ten Weeks on Train – Many Narrow Escapes". *The Record.* Volume XXII, Number 8. (May 31, 1918) 1 & 8.

"Miss Olmsted to Speak". 1945. *The Fulton Patriot".* (June 28, 1945)

"Miss Olmsted Will Address D.A.R. Meeting". 1944. *Geneva Daily Times.* (January 17, 1944) 7.

"Mrs. Emma Olmsted Succumbs to Illness". 1943. *The Record,* Sodus, NY. Volume XLVI, Number 45. (February 18, 1943) 1.

"National Archives Catalog: American Red Cross Historical Nurse Files." 1978. *Collection ANRC: Records of the American National Red Cross.* (February 12, 1978). File 1 of 2, pages 1-154 and File 2 of 2, pages 1-140. https://catalog.archives.gov/search?page=1&q=katherine %20Olmsted. *Note- scanned file is mislabeled as Kathleen M. Olmstead, however contents clearly state Katherine M. Olmsted. Reported to National Archives June 11, 2023.*

*Normandy Inn Menu.* 1943. During Katherine Olmsted's ownership (1943).

*Normandy Inn Menu.* 1960. During Katherine Olmsted's ownership (1960).

*Normandy Inn Scrapbook and Autograph Books.* Creator Unlisted. Maintained by Rita Kilpatrick. (viewed 2013 & 2023).

Norris, Chef Dorothy. 1984. "Cooking Corner: The Tastes of the Holidays: The Normandy Inn Ice Cream Cookie". *The Record*, Sodus, NY. (December 27, 1984) 3.

"Nothing to Fear" FDR Episode 1. Aired May 31, 2023. *History Channel.* history.americanhistory/biography. (May 31, 2023).

Olmsted, Anna Wetherill. Circa 1967. "The Story of An American Red Cross Nurse". *Self-published pamphlet* (circa 1967) 1-19.

Olmsted, Katherine. 1945. "That Cordon Bleu Touch". *New York Herald Tribune.* (June 17, 1945)

Olmsted, Katherine. 1963. "Business Summary, Normandy Inn". (September, 1963)

"Prevention of Accidents in Home & on Farm". 1943. *Syracuse Herald Journal.* (March 24, 1943)

"Record Jr.". 1930. *The Record*, Sodus, NY. (September 12, 1930) 8.

"Recordings". 1925. *The Record*, Sodus, NY. (December 25, 1925) 4.

"Recordings". 1926. *The Record*, Sodus, NY. (March 19, 1926) 4.

"Recordings". 1927. *The Record*, Sodus, NY. (March 25, 1927) 4.

"Recordings". 1931. *The Record*, Sodus, NY (December 4, 1931) 3.

"Recordings". 1965. *The Record*, Sodus, NY. (February 18, 1965) 4.

Russell, Christina. 2009. "Where to Eat or Maybe Not: The Normandy Inn". *The Sun & Record*, Sodus, NY. (January 15, 2009) 6.

Sanford, Terri & Atkins, Erin. 2023. Interview by Pamela Lee. May 16, 2023.

"Series Cooking Lessons offered by Katherine Olmsted".1942. *Syracuse Herald American.* (Jan 18, 1942 – Feb 4, 1942) 13.

"Sodus Centre". 1927. *The Record*, Sodus, NY. (June 10, 1927) 6.

Sodus Town Clerk. 1964. "Death Certificate, Katherine Olmsted." (April 7, 1964).

Splint, Sarah Field. 1920. *The Art of Cooking and Serving.* Procter & Gamble, Crisco Promotional Cookbook (circa 1920) 134.

"The Normandy Inn: A Gourmet's Paradise". 1975. *The Record*, Sodus, NY. (September 25, 1975) 2.

Unknown former diner, commentary given to Pamela Lee. May 2023.

VanWormer, Emma. 1947. "Normandy Inn has Old World Atmosphere: Quaintness of Sodus Restaurant Attracts Visitors from Start". *Syracuse Herald American.* (July 27, 1947) 24.

Wallington Cobblestone Schoolhouse Restoration Committee. 1982. *Arms' Crossroads-Wallington.* Lyons, NY: Wilprint, Inc. 68-83.

Wayne County Clerk. 1964. *Wayne County Clerk Records: Libor 536.* "Recorded Last Will and Testament". Grantor Katherine M. Olmsted: Grantee Anna Wetherill Olmsted. Executor Wayne County Surrogate's Court. (September 10, 1964). 520.

Wayne County Clerk. 1965. *Wayne County Clerk Records: Libor 572.* "Recorded Sale of Land". Grantor Anna Wetherill Olmsted: Grantee Dominic D'Ercole. (December 16, 1965). 841.

Wayne County Clerk. 1999. *Wayne County Clerk Records: Libor 961.* "Recorded Sale of Land". Grantor Dominick D'Ercole: Grantee Rita A. Kilpatrick and Michael K. Wasson. (February 16, 1999). 748.

Wayne County Clerk. 2020. *Wayne County Image Mate online.* "Recorded Sale of Land". James Hoyt purchased 7639 Ridge Road, Sodus from Rita Kilpatrick and Michael Wasson. (October 16, 2020). https://wayne.sdgnys.com/propdetail.aspx?swis=544289&printkey =07011700003555410000

Wayne County Clerk. 2022. *Wayne County Image Mate online.* "Recorded Sale of Land". Terri Sanford and Erin Atkins purchased 7639 Ridge Road, Sodus From James Hoyt. (January 24, 2022).https://wayne.sdgnys.com/propdetail .aspx?swis=544289&printkey=07011700003555410000

Webster, Ian. "Value of $1 from 1932 to 2023". Official Data Foundation/Alioth LLC. https://www.in2013dollars.com/us/inflation/1932?amount=1
(March 2023)

Williams, Miriam J. 1937. "Neighborly Normandy Inn". *The Farmer's Wife: local Magazine.* (June 1937).

"Women Support 6,500,000 Families, Miss Todd Asserts". 1950. *Buffalo Evening News*. (June 9, 1950) 20.

# Coming Soon!

## PREQUEL

Miss Olmsted's Nursing Adventures

Discover Miss Olmsted's early career in Nursing and join her for an adventure of a lifetime in Europe, first as a Red Cross Nurse during World War I and later as the Director of Nursing, League of Red Cross Societies in Geneva, Switzerland and Paris, France.  Look for the prequel in EARLY of 2024.

**Pamela Lee and
husband Rich Lee**

Pamela Lee lives with her husband Richard on Tigerlily Farm and they garden avidly. A talented mathematician, Pam daylights as a banker, which helps pay the bills. She also enjoys drawing, painting, sewing and crafting. Her newfound joy is researching and writing books.

Back cover image, Normandy Inn Mural believed to have been painted by Katherine Olmsted. Photo taken by Pamela Lee 2023, courtesy of Terri Sanford and Erin Atkins, building owners.